BEYOND the SCANDALS

"Unflinching in his sense of justice and sensitivity to victims, Lloyd Rediger nevertheless steadfastly moves beyond condemnation of perpetrators to an insightful analysis of sexual abuse dynamics— with particular reference to clergy roles. Crucially, he helps us see all of these phenomena in light of that healthy, joyous sexuality which characterizes divine and human generativity. As a richly experienced clinician and pastor to pastors, Rediger has given us an eminently useful and timely volume on clergy sexuality."

—JAMES B. NELSON, PROFESSOR EMERITUS OF CHRISTIAN ETHICS
UNITED THEOLOGICAL SEMINARY OF THE TWIN CITIES

"Rediger . . . here offers a wise book, *Beyond the Scandals,* on how the ecumenical church can finally begin to move beyond sexual noteriety to healing and health."

—*NATIONAL CATHOLIC REPORTER*

Other titles in

PRISMS

BEYOND the SCANDALS

A Guide to **Healthy Sexuality** *for* **Clergy**

G. Lloyd Rediger

FORTRESS PRESS

Minneapolis

BEYOND THE SCANDALS
A Guide to Healthy Sexuality for Clergy

Scripture quotations are from the New Revised Standard Version Bible, copyright © 1989 by the Division of Christian Education of the National Council of the Churches of Christ in the USA and used by permission.

The story and some of the material used in chapter 10 are taken from my book *Fit to Be a Pastor: A Call for Physical, Mental, and Spiritual Fitness* (Louisville: Westminster John Knox, 2000). Used by permission.

Cover design: Brad Norr

ISBN 0-8006-3613-9

The paper used in this publication meets the minimum requirements of American National Standard for Information Sciences — Permanence of Paper for Printed Library Materials, ANSI Z329.48-1984.

Manufactured in the U.S.A.
07   06   05   04   03   1   2   3   4   5   6   7   8   9   10

To pastors who practice the integrity of our calling,

To the victim-survivors of those who don't,

To dedicated advocates and healers

who minister to the dark side

of organized religion

CONTENTS

Part Three Healthy Sexuality

PREFACE

DURING MY OVER TWENTY-FIVE YEARS as a pastoral counselor to clergy and their families, I have been privileged to see the major changes in spiritual leadership from inside the minds and hearts of ministers, priests, and rabbis themselves. The most traumatic of these has been the recent widespread acknowledgment of moral malfeasance of approximately one-fourth of American clergy (Fortune 1997, 14). Some are only dabbling in sexual misconduct, but far too many have allowed boundary violations to become a way of life. Through media accounts, the churchgoing public has come to recognize the significance of this dark side of organized religion. And to their credit, religious organizations and denominations have done urgent work to devise codes of conduct and ethical retraining for clergy. But in some ways, we still don't get it; we have not fully confronted the realities, consequences, and implications of sexual abuse in church, synagogue, and temple.

The deepest roots and greatest ramifications of this crisis lie in religious life itself. For centuries, organized religion has treated human sexuality as a problem to be fixed rather than a creative, spiritual gift from God. Centuries of theology and policy in institutionalized religion have tried to emasculate and defeminize sexuality, hoping it would go away. But sex doesn't go away. It is a natural, hormonal, and relational dynamic of our lives and even of our spirituality. Human sexuality is a generative, caring gift from our Creator, and sex is our individual and shared stewardship of this gift. In this sense, organized religion does not *have* a problem with sexuality and sex; organized religion itself *is* the problem. For all the enormous good that religion and personal faith bring to the global family, we are in some ways still back in the Garden of Eden trying to sew fig leaves together to cover our shame. We can do better than this.

These broad statements are not intended as an insensitive sermon. Rather, they are the pained pleadings of one who has seen the devastation of sexual abuse up close—as a minister and counselor who has worked with countless abusers, victims, families, and denominational leaders concerning these troubling issues. I join many others in a wake-up call to churches and clergy and seminaries about understanding and managing our sexuality. And I hope to help amplify the cries of victim-survivors and to call on the church-at-large for justice, integrity, and realistic moral guidance from spiritual leaders.

This book is written with visionary hope that it can serve as a textbook for understanding the scope of our sexual complexities and the joyful exploration of our sexual spirituality. My strenuous efforts have been supported and enhanced by valued colleagues, experts, and companion pilgrims. Yet for this book to serve its purpose, an interactive process is necessary. Interspersed in these pages are also a number of questions, suggested exercises, and opportunities to discuss the behavior of the persons in the case studies.

Beyond the Scandals has three sections, which, though they may be artificial divisions, are intended to focus attention on different phases of our struggle with human sexuality and its spiritual dimensions. The first section (chapters 1–2) explores the contemporary scene of scandal and the metamorphosis of the role of the clergy. Chapter 1 reviews the media events that have shaped our consciousness concerning this latest wave of clergy sex scandals, and it compares the conditions and learning from the scandals of the 1980s with present conditions. Chapter 2 highlights the subtle yet deep transformations of the identified role of clergy in society. Interviews and conversations with Protestant, Catholic, and Jewish leaders, along with clergy from many ethnic contexts and of both genders, indicate the significance of these challenges and the difficulties of changing traditional clergy roles to meet them.

The second section (chapters 3–7) pulls back the curtain on the activities of the perpetrators and a defensive religious hierarchy, over against the victim-survivors and dismayed parishioners. It is an attempt to understand the specific dangers, patterns, and consequences of specific kinds of clergy sexual misconduct. Chapter 3 offers story-telling as a way to understand the subtleties and potentialities (especially transference-countertransference) in pastor-parishioner relationships. In my experience counseling is still the dynamic of pastoring where clergy are most at-risk and colleague-parishioners most vulnerable. Even though we have known about this phenomenon for so long, its temptations are still the threshold of many boundary violations. The interactive analysis after the story is designed as a self-review of competence in understanding and managing these encounters. Chapter 4 probes the dark, secret world of the pedophile molester, with cases that provoke dismay and anguish. The abuse of children, especially by church pastors, is the most tragic kind of sexual abuse that can be imagined. In addition to the appalling victimization of innocent children, there are families of the children who are disbelieving or enraged, and there are clergy perpetrators who are mentally impaired, addicted, or victims themselves of distorted understandings of sex and sexuality. Interventions and therapies for such cases are discussed.

The world of the sexual predator, rapist, and sex addict is explored in chapter 5. These abusers do not typically target children and are often less mentally impaired than the pedophile. But they live a life organized around sexual exploitation, seduction, and titillation. Personality disorders are common in this category of abuser; therefore, diagnostic classifications are compared with research and experiential characteristics. Stalking is noted in this category because of persistence and disruptiveness of this behavior. This shadowy type of predator is now being studied more carefully, due to celebrity encounters and recognition by professionals of the prevalence of this disorder. Chapter 6 delves into the "dissonant" types of sexual behavior, such as the paraphilias, sexual harassment, and the latest form of hardcore pornography, cybersex. These behaviors differ from abusive and exploitative behaviors in that they are typically less abusive, often practiced without a partner, yet are a dominating and potentially destructive aspect of the practitioner's life. Special attention is paid both to cybersex and sexual harassment because cybersex has become a sexual epidemic, and sexual harassment is so commonly accepted and poorly understood. Chapter 7 focuses on victim-survivors, from children to adults to whole congregations. A glossary of important terms and concepts is presented to highlight the unique sufferings of sex abuse victims, and the long-term effects, even if victims progress from helplessness to rage and vengeance, and on to surviving with a good prognosis. I then examine the controversy over forgiveness and reconciliation. I review and compare therapeutic modalities and summarize typical denominational protocols for managing clergy sexual misconduct. It is in chapters 3–7 that I draw also on my earlier work in *Ministry and Sexuality* (Rediger 1990).

The third and final section (chapters 8–10) is a prophetic exploration and celebration of healthy sexuality and its possibilities. It attempts to place clergy sexuality in a fresh psychological, theological, and pastoral framework. In chapter 8, the natural motivations of human beings are explored in what is termed Agendas of Human Behavior, and I show how these can distort or normalize expressions of sexuality. Contemporary ethics are discussed, with an emphasis on the now nearly universal dominance of consequential ethics over the more traditional ethics of absolute belief systems. In addition, the American attitude of entitlement is shown to be a special deviation from the traditional American philosophy of life, with serious implications for sexual lifestyles. Then the historic concept of conscience is recognized as a unique dynamic in human sexual behavior. Chapter 9 moves into a discussion of healthy sex and sexuality, emphasizing the importance of understanding the difference between these two concepts and their interdependence. Definitions basic to healthy sexuality are examined. I also present a set of theological syllogisms to identify and catalyze emerging theologies regarding the sexuality of God, human beings, and all of creation. Significant issues of sexuality are then related to theology and clinical experience, such as gender differences, the euphoric pleasures of sex, the global epidemic of HIV/AIDS, self-sex, and gay-lesbian sex. Intimacy is highlighted as the key emotional-relational experience of healthy sexuality. Chapter 10 tells the healing story of a competent pastor who explores the wrong side of sex and sexuality, with nearly disastrous results. But with the aid of a pastoral counselor he is able to see the warning signs, experience healing with his spouse and family, and become a model of healthy sexuality. The metaphor of biblical wholeness is then offered to show the dynamic, relational effects that occur when human persons convert to and pursue the biblical plan for wholeness of body-mind-spirit, including sexual wholeness. Finally, I raise the contemporary concept of fitness to highlight the positive possibilities of moving from sicknesses and sin, through healing and recovery, into a joyfully disciplined way of living as our Creator intended.

In the appendix I present an Inventory of Spirituality and Sexuality as a supplementary opportunity to find and examine the events, persons, and experiences that have shaped, limited, and inspired a personal, sexual spirituality.

The cases presented in this book are from my own counseling experience or reported to me by competent professionals. All cases have been altered in ways that disguise the identity of persons involved, without altering realities and issues. The story in chapter 3 is fiction based upon many cases I have worked with in my years as a pastoral counselor and as a confidential consultant to denominational officials.

This book is built upon the premise that sexual spirituality is the primary dynamic of God's creation. God's spiritual energy is expressed in sexuality throughout all of creation and is characterized by passion, creativity, vulnerability, and promise. When the human stewardship of sex is distorted, the powerful potential of spirituality becomes toxic. By God's gracious salvation, healing and wholeness are offered. This book is offered with a deeply concerned and hopeful prayer that God's Holy Spirit will guide us into a deeper understanding of the blessing of sexual spirituality. I am grateful to many people who have helped me with this project, as I explain in my acknowledgments (pp. 217–21).

Part One
Context

1.
UNDERSTANDING CONTEMPORARY
CLERGY SEX SCANDALS

What's Going On?

MEDIA HEADLINES AND REPORTS are drawing public attention to widespread clergy sexual misconduct. A spate of revelations, lawsuits, public recriminations, and even resignations of high-ranking clergy has revealed a systemic problem with clergy behavior and left a wake of tragically damaged lives. Even though sexual misconduct is rampant in our society, its occurrence among leaders of organized religion remains scandalous, while other occurrences, by inference, must seem like normal life in America. This incongruity is a significant indicator of the mores of North Americans and of their expectations concerning organized religion.

Meanwhile, the bastions of organized religion are under siege. For an attack on one entity in religion is an implied threat to others. Already assailed by secularism, the globalization of religion, and shrinking memberships, religion is now assaulted in its self-image and popular perception. Its time-worn theologies and politics of cathedral and hierarchy are exposed. Our anxiety and defensiveness leave us ill-prepared to celebrate and proclaim the fresh gospel of spirituality and generative sexuality in God's world.

In an earlier wave of clergy sex scandals (1970s–1980s), broad involvement was apparent. From Jimmy Swaggert, Jim Bakker, and lesser lights, through mainstream scandals, to high church, Orthodox, and Jewish malfeasances, came an impression that all clergy were under suspicion. In the more recent wave, the Catholic Church is the focus. This wave carries overtones of earlier shock and suspicion. The cumulative effect suggests serious questions for all of us: Whose problem is this? What information and trends are apparent? How should we interpret information responsibly? Where should we focus our attention and ministries? How can we prevent recurrences? Who will guide us into healthy understandings of the stewardship of human sexuality? This book endeavors to prompt reflection and answers to such questions.

Although the U.S. Catholic Church is the present focus of the clergy sex scandals, we recognize that this focus implicates all clergy and organized religion. We are all at-risk, and all must accept responsibilities for consequences of clergy sexual abuses. The mounting evidence has been so strong that the Catholic Church is on the defensive as seldom before in its American history. Its size, resources, doctrines, and hierarchical structure make it an attractive target for media, scandal-mongers, lawyers, and Protestants who wish to avoid responsibility for implications. The internal critics of the church have opportunities to both prate and be prophetic, while it leaders and adherents have occasion for shame and transformation.

Andrew Greeley warned of clergy risk and the vulnerability of laity often in reference to incoherence in Catholic doctrines and teachings regarding human sexuality and lax accountability in priestly roles. In *Crisis in the Church* (1979), he issued a broad warning: "Until the [Catholic] church begins to develop a new agenda for intimacy, evangelization will be nothing more than occupational rehabilitation for troubled bishops, priests and religious" (34).

In a new study of Catholic priests, commissioned by the National Federation of Priests' Councils, the volatile issues of homosexuality and celibacy are related to the current scandals. This study, conducted by sociologists Dean Hoge and Jacqueline Wenger of Catholic University, indicates that about one-quarter of priests surveyed believe there is a gay subculture in Catholic seminaries and in the priesthood, while attendant reactions suggest this is problematical. The vow of celibacy was also an issue of concern. We should note carefully that, although homosexuality and pedophilia are sometimes discussed together, there is no substantial evidence that gay priests are more likely to engage in sexual offenses than are heterosexual priests.

Opening such issues for discussion adds both candor and vulnerability for all concerned. With both allegations and confessions by prelates, as well as publicized court cases and settlements involving priests, there is less chance for denial and rationalization for any of us. Columnists from William Bennett and Cal Thomas to William Buckley and Ellen Goodman have offered critical analyses. The excesses of Fr. Paul Shanley's suggestion that sexual relationships between adult males and boys should be acceptable, and the radio broadcast of alleged sex acts in St. Patrick's Cathedral have precipitated outrage. The Associated Press indicates that an Internet database has been established (www.survivorsfirst.org) that lists 573 U.S. priests who have faced public accusations of child sex abuse since 1996. It also lists false charges brought against clergy. The influential newspaper the *Boston Globe* has been investigating Catholic clergy sexual misconduct for at least ten years. Recently it compiled its research and reportorial insights into a book entitled *Betrayal: The Crisis in the Catholic Church* (Carroll et al. 2002), which is a useful resource for putting clergy sexual misconduct in an understandable context.

An important issue has been diminished in the outcry against the sexual abuse of boys by priests in the Catholic Church. No less an authority on such issues than Richard A. W. Sipe was quoted in the *Boston Globe* as saying that he estimates that twice as many priests are involved with females as with males (Paulson 2002).

Paul Baier, founder of www.survivorsfirst.org, referred to above, calls for thoughtfulness in interpreting such figures. They should be compared with the 90,000 priests who have served in the past generation, not just the 46,000 now serving. This suggests that the 2,100 priests with claims against them are approximately 2.3 percent of priests. With such public and internal pressures, the Catholic Church is forced to defend itself or become open in its self-revelations.

Yet voices of caution have been heard warning of overreaction and violation of priests' civil rights, led by Pope John Paul during his World Youth Day address in Toronto, July 28, 2002. The Boston Priests' Forum also urged Cardinal Bernard Law, then archbishop, to clarify priests rights. And as of this writing, Bishop Wilton Gregory, President of the U.S. Conference of Catholic Bishops, indicated that it is striving for unity as it reviews the latest communications from the Vatican confirming the rights of accused priests. When victim-survivor groups hear such warnings, they worry that the church may remain more protective of priests and the hierarchy than responsive to abuse and suffering and to widespread loss of trust in institutionalized religion. Many now see clergy sex scandals contributing to a general questioning of religious faith and to the secularizing of society.

Lay movements in Catholicism are finding a voice and empowering themselves in what they call a righteous crusade by demanding openness and reform in the hierarchy and by acquiring potency in local governance. Due to the shortage of priests, laypersons and deacons are participating in services and liturgies with increasing responsibilities. There are now both an independent national review board and parish review boards investigating, reviewing, and advising on priestly scandals and church governance. Such lay involvement was unthinkable a generation ago. Some high ritual, hierarchically governed denominations tend to see lay movements as "essentially an outside intrusion," as a bishop remarked recently, while others welcome them.

Presently this movement is empowered not only by the usual critics and dissidents but also by a majority of the faithful. In a feature article on June 17, 2002, *Time* magazine quotes William V. D'Antonio, a researcher at Catholic University of America who found that 65 percent of "highly committed Catholics" supported "more democratic decision making" at the parish level, and 56 percent wanted more at the diocesan level. In the same article *Time* quotes James Muller, founder of Voice of the Faithful, a lay movement, as saying: "Two hundred years ago Americans gave representative democracy to the secular world. We're now attempting to do the same thing again—this time for the church" (Van Biema 2002, 57).

The tragedies of victims and survivors are receiving more sympathetic responses currently than was apparent in the earlier wave of clergy scandals. Marie Fortune, Gary Schoener, Archbishop Michael Sheehan, Nils Friberg, James Poling, Nancy Hopkins, I, and others, have insisted that organized religion recognize their painful plight and do justice on their behalf. This tragic issue has precipitated a nationwide recognition and more sensitive response to professional boundary issues, and the need for truth-telling in congregations. The personal stories of victim-survivors must be told, heard, and acted upon lest these injustices be compounded again.

Lawyers and the court system have had major influence on public perceptions of clergy malfeasance, the responses of religious leaders, and the behavior of clergy. Large though secret financial settlements for victim-survivors have emphasized the reality of civil and criminal abuses. Church insurance policies, codes of clergy conduct, and treatment plans for victim-survivors have been rewritten in response to litigation and threats of bankruptcy.

Other segments of organized religion also have major problems with clergy sexual misconduct. In the earlier wave of clergy sex scandals, the media and legal focus was on Protestant denominations. Enough allegations and criticisms are occurring beyond the Catholic Church to remind all of organized religion that clergy sexual misconduct continues, and that more abuse cases from the past are likely to emerge. The media's focus on Catholicism highlights priestly misconduct with children and youth. Protestant scandals tend more toward male pastoral involvement with female counselees or co-workers. The Associated Press, in an article in the *Albuquerque Journal*, April 5, 2002, quotes Gary Schoener, a respected Minneapolis psychologist and researcher, as citing a "typical Protestant case" in which a male United Methodist minister had an affair with a woman who sought his counsel in her struggle with alcohol and emotional problems. A jury awarded $10 million in this case. A study of the Presbyterian Church (U.S.A.) covering eight states over six years found 17 cases filed against clergy, with 31 female victims and involving one minor. The response to allegations tends to be quicker in Protestantism, according to the Associated Press investigations.

Presiding Bishop of the ELCA (Evangelical Lutheran Church in America), Mark S. Hanson, writes in the June 2002 issue of *The Lutheran:*

> When synod bishops receive an allegation, they investigate promptly. When credible evidence to support a charge exists, a bishop typically seeks the pastor's resignation from the clergy roster. If the pastor refuses, disciplinary charges may be brought, which can then lead to removal from the roster. A panel elected by the synod and churchwide assemblies hears the evidence and renders a judgment. An appeal process is available.
>
> Care of victims is our first priority. Healing emotional scars, re-establishing the trustworthiness of the congregation as a safe place, and tending to their shaken faith are important in our response to victims.
>
> We also encourage the accused pastor and his or her family to receive professional help.

Mainline and evangelical Protestant denominations are quietly thankful that this wave of clergy scandals is focused on the Catholic priesthood. But allegations and suspicions of misconduct continue to trouble many denominational offices and parishes. Statistics documenting clergy sexual misconduct are notoriously difficult to compile and report. Some statistics from the first wave of such scandals are worth noting. A survey of four denominations done by Fuller Seminary in 1984 indicate that 38 percent of clergy have had sexual contact with parishioners, 12 percent engaged in sexual intercourse, and 76 percent knew of clergy colleagues who had sexual intercourse with a church member. A survey of ministers quoted in *Leadership* magazine (winter 1988) indicated that 12 percent of respondents admitted to sexual intercourse outside of marriage: 17 percent with a counselee, 5 percent with a staff member, 30 percent with a parishioner. A 1993 survey of Southern Baptist pastors, quoted in the *Journal of Pastoral Care*, recorded 14 percent of respondents as noting sexual behavior inappropriate for a minister, 5 percent having sexual contact with someone in their church, and 70 percent noting sexual contact by colleagues with members of that church. Equally ominous was the indication in this report that 80 percent of clergy respondents affirmed the absence of written guidelines or policies regarding sexual behavior by clergy. (These statistics are quoted in Fortune 1997.) More recent trends and allegations involve sexual harassment and internet pornography (these factors will be discussed in greater detail in chapter 6).

Contextual Insights

Sex doesn't go away. It is built into us, into society, into the planet. Even God is sexual—in the sense of generative. Sex is a dynamic chaos—part of the swirling mass of spiritual energy that constitutes the universe. It is unpredictable, yet constant. It is strength, pleasure, and creativity. It is volatile, vulnerable, and disastrous. It is mine . . . yours . . . ours . . . God's. Sex doesn't go away.

Many of us have lived through the so-called sexual revolution, spanning approximately from the two world wars to the present. Though human sexuality—global sexuality—is not new, in this era it has become a dynamic, expansive burst of awareness and expression we may accurately call an eruption rather than a revolution. For the passions and creativity of sexuality are generated deep within us. They churn within and spew out of us. We are learning that we explore sex at our own risk.

The contemporary wave of clergy sex scandals is a reverberation of the clergy misconduct and malfeasance that shocked us in the 1970s and 1980s. In fact, many of the current scandals are about abuse and malfeasance that occurred in that earlier period and were ignored or covered up till now. And these are all part of the general social convulsions and sea changes we call modernism and postmodernism.

In earlier times sex had boundaries, limits, and controls. Now freedom, access, and globalization seem to say anything is possible. And as taboos, superstitions, and traditions are discarded, we find a biochemical-social-spiritual environment for which we are ill-prepared. Clergy should be capable of leading the way through this revolution. We are not. In fact, we are as vulnerable (human) as anyone. And when we fall, something powerful and precious is lost. Therefore, our mandate is to learn how to manage and teach our personal and shared sexual stewardship. This learning must take place in authentic relationships, as well as in classrooms and isolated experiences. And it must become a studied challenge for theologians, denominational officials, and laity, as well as pastors. For traditional doctrines, policies, and roles are inadequate to manage contemporary sexuality.

What We Are Learning

The learning capacity of human beings is both phenomenal and illusionary. We see, stumble, create, and learn in the process. Yet what we learn does not necessarily translate into changed thinking and behavior. When dealing with such powerful and dynamic motivations as sexuality, we must continue to learn and monitor. When we think we have learned the hard lessons and that this will keep us from making familiar mistakes, we are in danger of self-deception. For we change incrementally, unless forced into trans-formation by a confluence of overwhelming experiences. This pattern applies to the sexual eruption. Anne Bathurst Gilson has called it "Eros breaking free" (Gilson 1995) James B. Nelson called it "embodiment" (Nelson 1978). So we look back on the earlier clergy sex scandals and see what we have learned, should have learned, and must now relearn in amplified forms. It is instructive to list and reflect on these learnings. For if we are dis-cerning, we may avoid some disasters and even generate a fresh theology, ethics, and experience of God's gift of sexuality.

We are learning that sexuality does not go away. Testosterone and estrogen are produced by our bodies continuously, unless impairment or aging intervene. We are typically not conscious of the effects of these powerful hormones and don't yet know all the effects. But we are learning that we must intentionally shift our management of these hormones from the amygdala (powerful emotional reactions) to the hippocampus (memory evaluation), and then, hopefully, to the prefrontal lobe for a cognitive (respon-sible) decision (see Goleman 1995 [chapter 2] for a description of this process). This may sound like biochemical jargon and manip-ulation. It is, however, a clinical description that we need to study, for our mental machinations are becoming known through brain-mind research. Even though sexual motivations often take place at a preconscious level, we can develop an awareness of excitations in our neural pathways and learn how to manage responses more consciously. We need to understand how our sexual motivations function if we want to avoid impulsive, irresponsible sexual behavior. For it is apparent that right beliefs and codes of conduct are not strong enough to maintain appropriate sexual boundaries when passion is high (more on this later).

We are learning the shock of sexual betrayal by designated spiritual leaders—pastors, denominational officials, seminary professors, pastoral counselors, and lay leaders. I still recall the dawning awareness of seminary professors who preyed on students and sexually harassed staff members and did not even try to hide it. At national conventions of church leaders and psychotherapists, "sleeping around" was a favored pastime for some. The precipitous rise in divorces among spiritual leaders reflected this trend. In my pastoral counseling with pastors and church officials, I worked with some who complained that denominational officials were interfering in their private lives when they tried to discipline sexual misconduct. Others experienced enormous guilt trips that led them to seek repentance and forgiveness in pastoral counseling appointments at my office. I was awed to see the consequences of sexual misconduct by spiritual leaders. Nationally known authors were writing books, I among them, trying to aid organized religion in sorting out these issues. The result was a notable flurry of conferences, study groups, and codes of conduct devised in denominational offices in an effort to repair and prevent damage. We are learning the meaning of boundaries and limits.

We are learning that when the elected, ordained leaders of organized religion are unwilling to clean up the sexual malfeasance in their venues, outsiders will not only protest but are now more likely to intervene. In the 1970s and 1980s organized religion was shocked by legal interventions in congregations, seminaries, and denominational offices. This was a valuable wake-up call that forced rethinking of the traditional "good ol' boys" way of administering organized religion. Clergy were forced to rethink their call and the accountability of their role. Laypersons were stunned into accepting a shared responsibility for the morality of organized religion and its designated leaders. Congregations, denominations, and clergy have learned they must now carry liability insurance that covers malpractice. We have benefited from this continuing threat of interventions when spiritual leaders lose a sense of moral responsibility. Yet it is apparent that awareness and codes of conduct have not yet resolved the clergy sexual misconduct predicaments.

We are learning the malfeasance that occurs when denominational leaders, seminary officials, and directors of religious agencies devote their energies to protecting these institutions rather than managing them toward fulfilling their mission of justice, integrity, and caring.

We are learning the enormity of pain and damage that clergy sexual malfeasance causes. For a short time (or is it still the perspective of some?) after the first wave of clergy sex scandals, it seemed easy to believe it was better not to pry into or talk about such matters except behind closed doors, and among those who could control information and responses. But we have learned that persons abused by clergy are frequently injured severely, with long-term damage. Often these victim-survivors were ignored, given perfunctory attention, warned to be silent, or "paid off" in some way. With the intervention of lawyers and the courts, such responses are less likely now. Moreover, we have learned that there are multiple victim-survivors in each instance—congregations, spouses, families, colleagues, along with the perpetrator. The church is malfeasant and hypocritical if it does not respond with competent caring and support.

We are learning that sexual misconduct of spiritual leaders takes multiple forms. Pedophilia and ephebophilia are especially tragic, as youthful lives and trust are violated. We also know that some personality disorders and addictions predispose one to sexual misconduct. And we know now that pastors, in particular, have unique opportunities to hide or camouflage their malfeasance, including the new and insidious opportunities to indulge in cyber-sex. Victim-survivors also are diverse, and their responses varied. There is no one simple formula for understanding or remedying these tragedies.

We have learned that the clergy role is fraught with at-risk occasions for malfeasance. The "star factor" (pedestal effect) plays a part in the clergy role. This is nearly the only profession where people gather regularly to listen to one person "declare the word of the Lord," along with sundry insights. Pastors are not thought of or treated like other persons. Deference, privilege, and power are usual in the role, which is heady stuff, even for those who deny it or do it poorly. The "intimacy factor" is also integral to the role. Pastors are allowed to know secrets and be more personal than laypersons. Such closeness can produce naïve trust, exemptions, and even seduction, for which many are ill-prepared. Yet typical intimacies of clergy are "half-intimacies." That is, the confidentiality and emotions are usually one-way, like co-dependencies. Further, the pastor's reputation depends on respect and integrity. Questions of immorality destroy clergy careers. Ideas of "free sex" and "open marriage," though more popular now, are incompatible with effective pastoring. We are reminded frequently that sex and love are not synonymous.

We have learned the three key words of pastoring: relationships, relationships, relationships. Pastoring is built upon relationships . . . healthy relationships. Effective pastors establish clear communications and caring interactions with congregational leaders and parishioners. For though there is a built-in authority and connectedness between pastor and parishioners, the relationship must be nurtured, lest it deteriorate. The pastor must build a support base that nurtures, supports, and holds all people accountable. Effective pastors encourage healthy relationships within the congregation, healthy relationships with the community, healthy relationships with God, and healthy relationships with our planet. We are learning the differences between healthy and unhealthy relationships, for when we do not, our relation-ships can seduce and trap us.

We have learned and are learning that our society—and most of the developed world—now lives according to an ethics of conse-quences rather than an ethics of beliefs. This is a paradigm shift in human relationships. Although organized religion still preaches and teaches theology and the practices of spirituality, it too now operates out of a set of pragmatic practices. An illustration is the reality of the business model as the basis of policy and adminis-trative decisions in denominations, congregations, and seminaries.

This ethics of consequences (EthCon) is more deeply entrenched in our thinking and practice than we may think. It is not all bad. However, EthCon is an enormous shift from what we imagine is the basis of our behavior and decision-making. We still recite our creeds and doctrines, but we break the speed limit whenever we need to, as long as no traffic officer is visible. We still enjoy lifestyles far beyond our real needs, although two-thirds of the global family lives in poverty and injustice. And more than a few of us practice our sexuality not according to our stated beliefs but according to what pleases us at the moment. We are learning that spiritual disciplines are the prescription for lost faith and confused ethics. For when we blend healthy beliefs and spiritually disci-plined motivations, we achieve healthy consequences. Healthy sex-uality is more deeply pleasurable and satisfying than "feel good" sexuality, with its consequential vulnerabilities and malfeasance.

What Is New This Time

The present eruption of clergy sex scandals includes all of the issues just listed. In addition, the following indicators suggest dis-turbing trends, as well as hopeful improvements related to our theme. Each of these indicators provides an opportunity for per-sonal reflection and/or group discussion.

Awareness is different this time. A general knowledge that a small but significant number of clergy have been and are involved in sexual misconduct is helping organized religion as well as society in general to put these scandals into a more realistic perspective. Our general awareness, however, still includes misconceptions, prejudices, and false assurances. Further, it is our focused and trained awareness that can use clergy sex scandals as an impetus to transform our theology, policies, and ministries. This means seminaries, denominational offices, and clergy groups must accept more responsibility to train and promote healthy sexuality. Training and promotion must now include laity. For sexual health is as important for congregants as for clergy.

Depreciation of commitment loyalty is almost a rite of passage in our society. The natural rebellion of youth now seems to occur for many adults as they strive for independence and control of their lives. Lifelong loyalty to an ethnic tradition, to a cause, or to professional honor was a more prominent principle in previous generations. Wearing slogan-emblazoned T-shirts or having an American flag rolled up in the garage is a sufficient residual of an age of loyalty for many. There is more freedom to shift loyalties often. Commitment to a relationship, a communal quest, or a belief system, though often given lip service, seems too great a sacrifice of individual freedom. Such social dynamics and attitudes contribute to moral breakdowns.

Demythologizing of tradition and policy continues in both religion and society. No institution, belief system, or policy is above scrutiny. Organized religion, in its many forms, must now accept examination and social demands for change, even as it continues to redefine its mission in guiding the human struggle for spiritual health.

Pronouncements, doctrines, and even the social mystique of religion's role in society no longer protect organized religion from the paradigm shifts and sea changes of this millennium. This continuing social transformation, which developed following World

War II, deeply affects religion's understanding and management of present clergy sex scandals. We are realizing that the tweaking of doctrines and policies is no longer adequate. Spiritual leadership demands transformation as a continuing process. This means public accountability, honesty and truth, a reformation of spiritual disciplines, and a transformation of organizational forms.

Codes of conduct are now part of nearly every denomination's policies and training. They have been tested and refined to meet clinical and legal requirements. Parishioners, however, still are not fully informed of these safeguards and guidelines. And many still think religious codes of conduct are for clergy only.

Assessment and therapies are better informed. The professional disciplines of mental health now presume the authority to diagnose and treat mental disorders in both individuals and human systems. Although psychology has tended to disregard religious traditions and spiritual dynamics, it has generated a broader understanding of how disordered and healthy minds work. And it offers valuable therapies that can modify unhealthy behavior patterns, aid in understanding the consequences of abuse, and assist in guiding human relationships and communities into prevention, justice, and health.

Legal trends and attitudes have changed, although laws are still much the same. Organized religion knows now that courts can intervene when civil or criminal laws are violated. Yet lawsuits often encumber our efforts to reform. American's love affair with litigation now has lawsuits, counter-lawsuits, serial lawsuits, and threats of lawsuits. This tends not only to frighten and distract, it diverts attention from repentance, forgiveness, reconciliation, and reverence in our stewardship of sexuality and justice. The moral laws of organized religion and civil decency no longer seem to offer viable alternatives to litigation.

Prominence for women in the workplace, professions, and athletics is enriching society and transfiguring organized religion. The feminine presence has new meanings and influences. There were

16,400 female pastors in 1983, compared to 43,542 in 1996 (see www.barna.org). Women now comprise about one-third of the seminary student population. Such sudden prominence for women has massive influence on the male population. Society must cope with increases in domestic violence, rape, and sexual harassment, even while celebrating female leadership. The effects of female prominence in church and synagogue are yet to be measured fully. (Research on the sudden influx of ethnic [non-Caucasian] clergy, their influence, and conduct, is even less developed than for women.)

Media influence in sexuality was a new influence in the earlier wave of clergy sex scandals. The drive for free expression, entertainment, and profit have now driven media into a central role in the understanding and expression of human sexuality. The constant prominence of sexual themes and models certainly feeds the already powerful libido of many. While we celebrate sexual freedom we must now live with the negative consequences of relatively undisciplined expressions.

Gay and lesbian issues are more prominent in this wave. For some, pedophilia and celibacy issues still raise specters of garbed prowlers and emasculated clergy roaming the halls of churches. In the worst cases, clergy sexual misconduct is nearly this heinous. But such cases should not be associated with gay-lesbian clergy, for there is no statistical correlation. The reality that some religious people can still blame gay and lesbian clergy for most of the clergy sex scandals is a reminder of organized religion's unfinished business in relating to homosexual persons. However, in recent years gay-lesbian persons have become more prominent in both public protests and in preaching, teaching, and modeling their perspectives on healthy sexuality and spirituality. This provides somewhat calmer opportunities to discuss problematic issues from both heterosexual and homosexual perspectives, without becoming enmeshed in prejudices, while we work to eliminate clergy sexual misconduct.

Cybersex is one of the most insidious new versions of sexual misconduct yet devised. Although its primary dynamic, pornography with masturbation, is not new, this computerized version provides secrecy, narcissistic gratification, addictive habits, diversion from healthy relationships and practices, and alienation from God's purposes for our sexuality. Since cybersex is so secretive, seductive, and interactive, organized religion must give serious attention to countering this evil with realistic teachings and practices of healthy, joyful sexuality.

Each of us is responsible for our own sexual sicknesses, healing, and health. No one can do these for us. No code of behavior, lawsuit, New Year's resolution, or escapism will suffice. Fortunately, a growing number of clergy are finding that physical-mental-spiritual fitness and healthy lifestyles are the basis for healthy sexuality.

Clergy sexual malfeasance has and is causing great pain and confusion. Yet, if we take time to understand it, such malfeasance can point us to the truth about human sexuality and to faithful spiritual leaders who model and teach healthy sexuality. "You will know the truth, and the truth will make you free" (John 8:32).

Summary

This chapter connects current clergy sex scandals with an earlier phenomenon. Present scandals have become media events, as newspapers, periodicals, television, and radio investigate and opine regarding significant factors, identities, and significance. Nondefensive comments and actions by religious leaders are needed in order to add appropriate perspectives from organized religion.

The earlier wave of clergy sex scandals and the present events are compared in order to provide a series of perceptions generated by organized religion while it learns the realities of clergy sexual misconduct.

Finally, a list of indicators suggests how this contemporary wave of scandals differs from and is similar to the first.

The issues sketched in this chapter will be discussed in more detail as they become significant themes in later chapters.

2. DIAGNOSIS: ABNORMAL

WHAT IS NORMAL for most people is not normal for pastors. What is normal for pastors is abnormal for many people. Therefore, in a sense, pastors are abnormal.

This shocking truth can be stated another way: Most pastors are normal. Pastors typically have normal joys and sorrows. They are human beings first and clergy second. Yet pastors must learn to speak, work, and think abnormally.

The Role of Pastor

Stated yet another way, the role of a pastor is abnormal. If pastors talked, worked, and thought like other people, they wouldn't be pastors. Is there a problem here?

Through many years of doing psychotherapy and consultations with clergy, I learned that when a pastor came to my office, I had at least two clients—one was the pastor and the other was the clergy role. A pastor is a living convergence of personhood and this professional role. This duality is not a problem; it is a learning and developmental issue for the pastor. The role of pastor, however, is problematic. For it is undergoing forced changes, with consequences as yet not well understood.

Human beings in general must deal with the need to function in several roles—student, parent, woman-man, professional, Christian, person of color, Jew, villain-hero, victim-survivor, believer-unbeliever, pastor-spiritual guide. We have distinct names for many roles, with duties and learnings attached to all of them. It is not just pastors who must cope with role-playing and personhood at the same time.

The role of pastor, however, is unique in significant ways. This uniqueness is important to the subject of this book, namely, clergy sexuality and the clergy role. Both have unhealthy and healthy versions. The role is so prominent that clergy sexuality is perceived and judged by it.

The clergy role is *sui generis,* for it is the only profession that wraps personal identity, professional identity, and religious all in the same package. Further, it already exists in the mind of most human beings, whether there is a pastor around or not. Responsibilities and mysteries are built into it, most of them reflecting deep needs and expectations. The Judeo-Christian tradition teaches that some members of the faith community are called by God and the community, and then vowed, to serve in spiritual leadership roles. The human being who accepts this role remains a human being but must find ways to meet the expectations of the role. An identifiable core of behaviors and responsibilities already exists for this role, yet each individual who fills it, and each individual who receives its ministrations, is unique, with a variety of talents and needs. Further, there are specific ethnic, gender, and faith traditions that influence both the fulfilling and the perception of the pastoral role.

When I begin to relate to a pastor in a confidential, professional way, I know that my first task is to discover the troubling experience of the person who has come for assistance. For the personal issue is the key, but the role is often the presenting factor. I learned this as a pastor, then I sorted out the dynamics in clinical training and my own psychotherapy. Yet throughout my years of ministry I am continually learning the unique dynamics that converge for a pastor and congregation when they relate to each other as both human beings and as role players in a faith community.

The role of pastor is a historic extension of the ancient role of shaman-medicine woman/medicine man. When people began to codify their religion, the role of mystical spiritual leader morphed into what the Jewish Bible portrays as patriarch (Abraham), charismatic leader (Moses), priest (Aaron), warrior king (David), and prophet (Elijah, Isaiah). In the Christian Testament priests and theologians were preeminent, with prophets, insurrectionists, and mystical healers in the background. Jesus broke into this mix as a combination of spiritual leadership roles, but quickly superseded these roles as "one who speaks with authority" and then "Son of Man/Son of God." He, of course, became the model for all subsequent spiritual leaders in the Christian tradition. Over the centuries that model has been modified to accommodate the limitations of mere mortals.

This shaman-to-Jesus role is the oldest role, outside of parenting, in human history—in spite of the claim of one other ancient profession. This role engulfs contemporary clergy the moment we are ordained. From then on we are different, set apart from normal persons. We are called into this role. We take vows and receive blessings that are different from what happens to normal people. We get a piece of paper to hang on our wall—different from what any other person hangs on their wall. And, unlike any other person, we stand in front of people at least once a week and purport to speak for God, while people sit and listen to us.

No one else does this—or if they do, it's still not the same as when we do it. People tell us private things—heavy stuff. And we are supposed to keep it secret, after we tell them how to handle the mess they're in. There is more: people ask us about God, how to get to heaven, what to do about their sins, how to live lives pleasing to God—or, if they don't ask us, they at least expect us to answer these questions in one hour on Sundays. Further, as we fill this role, people are relating to us through the clergy "mystique." They are sometimes reassured and often surprised when they get glimpses of our humanness.

Now add sexuality to all this. It's already there. And those who imagine clergy are not sexual, or not supposed to be, are part of a massive person-role problem. It's the role again. For human beings are just human beings. Sex is just sex. And the role of spiritual leader is just another role, unless we add the clergy mystique, the historic traditions and codifications, the spiritual presence of the Holy Trinity, and sex.

Note that throughout this book the terms sexuality and sex have related but different meanings. Sexuality is God's gift of relational generativity. Sex is the human thoughts and behavior that express the genital and intimate aspects of sexuality.

Sex and sexuality don't go away. They are part of God, creation, and humankind. And they are good. In fact, sex is a necessary dynamic of creativity and caring. Sex will give joy and passion to life. But it is potent. Use with care and thankfulness. Read the instructions.

We must intentionally include a major cluster of players in this clergy role mix, namely, seminaries, denominational offices, the hierarchies of organized religion, and communities of faith. I will discuss congregations later and leave an analysis of the first three to other writers, except for recognizing their presence and influence. I must, however, mention some of the inadequacies in this cluster, with a caveat that this is a perspective limited by the scope of this book. They are mentioned because of the influence they have on contemporary clergy sex scandals. Seminaries are still built and conceived around the academic model. However, some are setting up classes, providing counseling and training in sexuality, and offering supervision and mentoring that includes frequent study and discussion of human sexuality and how this fits with spirituality.

Denominational offices and the executives that lead them devote much of their time and resources to becoming efficient small (or large) businesses. The business model has become a driving force in the management of most aspects of organized religion. The first wave of clergy sex scandals forced them quickly to learn a few of the realities involved in combining human beings and the morphing clergy role. To their credit, they promptly owned part of the problem and spent considerable time writing codes of conduct for clergy. Enforcing these codes is a continuing problem, however, along with recognizing that lay persons are at least as big a part of the sex scandals as are pastors.

Codes of conduct and codes of ethics are related but are not the same. Codes of ethics spell out beliefs and accountability concerning a professional role. Codes of conduct are the specified behaviors and protocols for enforcing them. Conduct and ethics are sometimes blended in a single document or perspective. This may seem normal, but it can be confusing. For beliefs and conduct are manifested and treated in different ways.

The hierarchies of organized religion are an intriguing and now problematical part of our sex scandals. All organized religious groups have hierarchies, whether they recognize this or not. But they do not all look alike in outward appearance. There are conservative-liberal variations. There are ethnic-cultural variations. And, finally, there are beginning to be gender variations. In part, these hierarchies carry a powerful tradition of religious leadership, with various roles, codes, and spheres of influence. Contemporary media and legal entities are now forcing changes that did not occur in traditional religious setups. When we factor in the sea changes in global interactions and the outrage of victims and the faithful at the old order, the current clergy sex scandals seem to be a portent of massive paradigm shifts in organized religion. Similar changes are occurring in many sectors of human life.

I return now to the clergy in the role of client, who is in need of deeper understanding regarding the historic, primal needs he or she serves and the difficulties we encounter as we mix normal human-ness with the mystique of spiritual leadership. A prominent and often static aspect of the clergy role as lived by a particular pastor is normalcy. By normal, I mean the mental image a pastor has of how a pastor should think, act, and work. Although each pastor has ordinarily been trained in a version of the role of pastor, he or she interprets this version to fit her personal needs, experience, and expectations. The role of pastor comes in a variety of recognizable forms. Yet each pastor's version is unique in some ways.

"Normal" is important in our society, and in any society, organization, or human relationship. It is the unconscious and conscious consensus about what is appropriate behavior and lifestyle for those accepted in the group. Those who violate its standards are punished, and those who live by them are rewarded. Any adult in the group has typically learned and accepted this version of nor-malcy and will usually discipline themselves to follow it. The true power of normal, however, occurs at the unconscious level, where the internalized normal behavior pattern becomes a regulator of thinking and behavior. A person living the acceptable normal behavior and lifestyle will feel comfortable, and the person violat-ing this standard will feel uncomfortable, and then return to nor-mal behavior, unless she can give herself a comfortable reason for violating the standard. This concept of normal will be discussed more fully in a later chapter on health and fitness.

Another prominent dynamic of the clergy role can be called the "star factor." This is the constant prominence of the pastor's pres-ence and name in a congregation's identity and programs. His name appears on the outdoor bulletin board. Her name appears at the top of the church stationery and Sunday worship guides. The pastor leads worship, presides at church meetings, performs funerals and weddings, and is usually known in the community. He or she often refers to the congregation as "my congregation." The pastor is "up front" constantly. And now with the business model operative in congregations, the pastor must function as manager or CEO. This star factor goes along in the stores, on the golf course, even at home. A pastor can accentuate the star factor or minimize it. She cannot eliminate it.

Advantages and disadvantages accrue to the office of pastor from the star factor. Some advantages are the "open door" attitude in which parishioners usually welcome their pastor into their homes and personal lives; the "authority" factor in which the pastor is presumed to know more about God and the workings of the church than other persons; and for pastors who are confident and groomed, there is even the unique brand of sexual attractiveness that for some embellishes the clergy role. This factor, of course, can lead to sexual offenses for pastors who do not understand and practice professional boundaries.

Disadvantages that accompany the star factor include the 24/7 schedule, the necessity of playing the role in home and community even when preferring just to be human, the expectation of always pleasing your fans, the blame for failures of the congregation, the elevated self-image of stardom, the poor pay and temporary ego trips, and suffering the public shame for real or perceived sexual malfeasance. The star factor is like your shadow—smaller or larger than your physical presence, depending on where the light is coming from.

Throughout this discussion we need frequent reminders that while we concentrate on the problems and scandals of spiritual leadership, we also live with an enormous history of benefits to humanity provided by the faithful and at times even prophetic spiritual leadership of clergy. We need only mention a history of establishing schools, hospitals, and spiritual guidance paradigms. More recently, significant leadership was provided by clergy in the civil rights movement. Now advocacy for peace is reemerging. Some of us pray that a national crusade for healthy sexuality and healthy lifestyles will emerge.

The role of pastor reflects all these strengths and weaknesses, with the addition of the personal touch a pastor brings to a local community of faith and the larger community. The present sex scandals demonstrate the great reservoir of trust and appreciation that still exists to help empower this role. It is the malfeasance, the violation of this goodwill, that is shocking society, eroding personal faith, and victimizing so many who needed the ministrations of clergy. Even in the face of such destructive scandals, we can find some reassurance in the reality that approximately 80 percent of clergy still function competently and faithfully.

What then goes wrong when seemingly moral, spiritual leaders violate professional boundaries? In a recent interview, Archbishop Michael Sheehan of the Archdiocese of Santa Fe, an early leader in developing a model for managing priestly scandals effectively, said that one issue is predominant when priests perpetrate sexual abuse: "They lose their prayer life. . . . No one can sustain the sacrificial life of celibate pastoral ministry without deep spiritual disciplines." In other interviews I found spiritual leaders of evangelical denominations also emphasized the urgent need for spiritual disciplines as pastors face the challenge of blending authentic humanity with dedicated spiritual leadership.

Reverend Dr. Barney Self, Leader Care Counselor for the Southern Baptist Convention, affirmed this same need for spiritual disciplines among clergy. He added that local congregations, which are autonomous, must find better ways of spelling out and supporting acceptable moral ethics for their pastors.

Louis McBurney, M.D., along with his spouse, Melissa, built a model of evangelical psychiatric care for pastors and their spouses at Marble Retreat, in Colorado. In a most cordial interview with him and Melissa at their scenic retreat house, I heard an insightful description of how devastated pastoral lives and marriages can be healed, and how spiritual disciplines can be lived in realistic ways. I especially value Dr. McBurney's personal prayer with me at the close of our extended conversation, in which he laid his hand on my head and prayed for a special blessing on this book.

The Reverend Homer Ashby, Ph.D., Professor of Pastoral Care at McCormick Theological Seminary in Chicago, has developed a curriculum and mentoring process in which professional boundary issues are studied. He also hosted my interviews with African American religious leaders in the Chicago area. These interviews noted the special issues involved in the paternal model of pastoring in some black congregations. For while black denominations still emphasize enthusiastic spirituality, racist dynamics in most American communities have kept black churches separated into enclaves in which spiritually and morally healthy pastors try to sustain healthy congregations. Yet it is not uncommon, Ashby notes, for promiscuous pastors to replicate some of the sexual offenses typical of former plantation culture. A strong movement among African American women churchgoers is now working to expose and transform malfeasant pastors, assist victim-survivors, and empower churches not only to fight sexual abuse in congregations but also to eliminate similar violence in the home.

Father Richard Olona, pastor of Albuquerque's largest Catholic congregation (largely Hispanic) and chancellor of the Archdiocese of Santa Fe, discussed his enlightened view of pastoral ministry coupled with celibacy in a long conversation with me in his office. When I asked about the impact of the priest scandals, he shook his head slowly and looked deeply pained. The shock of headline scandals was an extension of the pain in this parish as it lost its beloved pastor to the scandal a couple of years prior to the more recent exposés. There has been much weeping, praying, and confusion as parishioners had to think differently about the priesthood and their focus on the priest's presence in their midst. Father Olona said the most positive outcome so far is the shifting of parishioners' attention from the priest to God and the sacraments again. Then he told of reorganizing his parish around lay leadership, so he could attend to the sacraments and spiritual needs. In this lively and cordial interview I heard a description of a revitalized, traditional model of pastoring that allows a priest to devote his energies to spiritual needs and celebrations and to his own spiritual disciplines. In Father Olona's view this eliminates the burnout track followed by priests who feel a need to micromanage the parish, leaving inadequate time and energy for healthy humanness. He noted his experience as a supervisory leader indicating that priests who develop such a model in life and ministry are much less prone to sexual offenses.

Rabbi Arthur Gross-Schaeffer, Associate Professor of Law and Ethics, College of Business, Loyola Marymount University, Los Angeles, in recent conversations and writings has been supporting a movement in Reform Judaism to "break the silence," regarding the exposing of rabbinical boundary violations, and the hidden pain and injustice to victim-survivors. He provides legal guidelines to encourage openness in investigation and stopping the abuses. His advocacy for eliminating sexual harassment in the workplace as well as in congregations is a valuable model.

In the 1980s, when the clergy sex scandals first became headline news, there was a lingering question about whether this phenomenon was a pervasive issue or simply a case of a few aberrant pastors. Since then it has been clear that approximately one-fourth of clergy have been or are involved in sexual misconduct of some sort. We are searching now for the causative factors and the context to explain why moral leaders violate moral standards in significant numbers. Some strong clues are emerging.

Insight 1: External and internal forces are making sex a prominent problem in society and in organized religion. In chapter 8 some of these external forces are highlighted. The example used is the paradigm shift from an ethics of belief (EthBel) to an ethics of consequences (EthCon). This shift tends to make every person his/her own ethical reference point, and often leads to individuals doing whatever "seems like a good idea at the time." The internal forces contributing to clergy sexual malfeasance are many, but the one highlighted in chapter 6 is the system of unconscious psychological motivations I called "agendas for human behavior." These tend to keep us searching for better management of three dominant internal motivations.

Insight 2: A monumental change has been and is occurring in the clergy role, causing role confusion among many clergy and consternation among parishioners. When the role changes, the person trying to fill it loses traditional reference points. In striving to meet both traditional and emerging expectations, an internal stress is generated that then complicates the lifelong effort to be the best person I can be, in or out of the role. This internal stress is producing an identifiable syndrome of maladies in significant numbers of clergy. Role confusion, burnout, depression, and sexual misconduct have become a predictable pattern for clergy who do not keep themselves healthy in body-mind-spirit. The maladies reinforce each other, making it difficult to deal with these personal maladies, as well as fulfill a role that is no longer clear.

Insight 3: The developing dominance of diversity and secularism (post-Christian thinking) and the emergence of alternative forms of spirituality are threatening to force organized religion into massive changes. One of our responses is reestablishing a redemptive, empowering, and credible system of religious beliefs while including pragmatic applications, as Jesus did. Many believers and pastors have fallen into a state of chronic religion. This is a form of religion that has deteriorated into a set of behavioral habits and rote beliefs, with little inspiration or creativity.

These insights are being developed throughout this book. But now some informative evidence can be explored to guide our search for remedies, prevention, and health.

Frequent Clergy Maladies

Research done for the Wisconsin Conference of Churches and the Minnesota Council of Churches in the 1990s suggests a curious dynamic among pastors of local congregations. (The Wisconsin survey was done with the assistance of Robert Bendiksen, Ph.D., Professor of Sociology, University of Wisconsin–LaCrosse, and a grant from the United Methodist Foundation; the Minnesota survey was done with the assistance of the Reverend Dan Bruch, Ph.D., Professor of Sociology, Concordia College, St. Paul, and a grant from the Minnesota Council of Churches.) The high stress levels reported by many (74 percent), must be compared to an overlapping number who report feeling normal and enjoying the life of a pastor (78 percent feel their "spiritual life is not deteriorating"; 75 percent "seldom have conflicts"; 70 percent feel "normally energetic"; 64 percent report "few financial difficulties"). Another issue that occurs in much research on clergy is the "halo effect," in which pastors apparently try to present an exaggerated positive image. This is likely in the seeming discrepancy between those reporting normal comfort levels and yet expressing high levels of stress in later questions. It is likely also as 63 percent of pastors in the survey indicated knowing colleagues who had engaged in sexual misconduct, while 5 percent of them reported their own sexual misconduct.

This unexpected outcome (unexpected by those of us who deal with clergy problems regularly) is confirmed in research done in the Duke Divinity School's "Pulpit and Pew Project," directed by the Reverend Jackson Carroll, Ph.D. This survey indicates that 74 percent of respondents reported they were very satisfied in their present situations and felt only moderate levels of stress. Approximately two-thirds felt "loved and cared for." These findings are nearly identical with my research.

The high stress level among pastors tends to set them up for four frequent maladies in the clergy population.

1. The first, though not most frequent, is role confusion. This is now frequent in other professions where requirements and expectations are changing significantly. For pastors, role confusion, as used here, is a mix of temporary or continuous doubts, severe criticism, career failures, faith crises, divorce, mixed expectations, and loss of normal competence. Role confusion can result in and from burnout, when there is not adequate energy available to sort out career dilemmas.

2. A second common malady is burnout, a consequence of expending more energy than is taken in, over a long or highly stressed period of time (see Rediger 1982). In my research for the Wisconsin Conference of Churches and Minnesota Council of Churches, mentioned earlier, 74 percent reported, "I always feel I should be doing more." (This question and percentage are nearly identical for respondents in a study of burnout done by Austin Theological Seminary in 2000.)

Burnout develops from such feelings and the continuing urgency of trying to catch up with "unfinished business." Burnout typically follows periods of church conflict, competing commitments, feelings of incompetence for required duties, severe personal criticism, marital and family problems, congregational struggles, career disappointments or transitions, frustrations from illness, impairment, and aging, and guilt trips consequential to sexual misconduct.

3. High stress living often sets us up for the third malady, depression. One characteristic of depression is low energy. Other frequent characteristics are unusual mood swings, irritability, sleeplessness or abnormal drowsiness, lessening or excessive appetite, low self-esteem, and lessening of libido (although sometimes situational depression can induce irresponsible sexual behavior). The depression that typically accompanies burnout is termed exogenous, meaning it may pass when circumstances improve. Long periods of burnout, however, may trigger biochemical or

genetic (endogenous, long-term) depression. For further information on depression, consult Johnson and Johnson 2002.

A major concern in this chapter is the high stress/burnout malady so common among pastors. One prescription for this malady is wiser management of energy. Since many of us do not pay close attention to where our energy comes from and where it goes, taking some time to recognize this energy process has been valuable to many clergy who attend my seminars.

4. The fourth clergy malady that is now seen frequently is the focus of this book, clergy sexual misconduct. This set of inappropriate or abusive behaviors is also called "clergy sexual malfeasance" (violation of professional trust and commitments), "sexual offenses" (sexual behavior that causes harm or damage), and "boundary violations" (intentionally or inadvertently exceeding the limits of sexual discretion, or abusing trust and personhood of another human being). Clergy sexual misconduct may be caused or abetted by the other three maladies discussed above—role confusion, burnout, and depression. For any of these can generate low resistance to temptation, miscalculation of consequences, denial of true motivations, and forgetfulness regarding professional boundaries. However, contributing causes such as these should never be allowed as excuses.

Women Clergy
and the Role of Pastor

Women are different from men in real life, in fantasy, and in the pulpit. This fact and its impact are noticeable now and must be factored into all issues related to organized religion. Over the last fifty years, the number of women in or preparing for ministry as pastors has increased approximately 250 percent (this is small in comparison to the increase of women as physicians and lawyers).

Approximately one-third of seminary students are women, and 12–15 percent of pastors serving parishes are women. All these statistics are trending upward. (These statistics are from Lindner 2002 and from Carroll et al., 1983.)

Statistics on numbers and percentages of women related to organized religion do not yet have the long-term reliability common to statistics for men. Yet there is a growing body of anecdotal and case-study material from women's sources, and from those of us who have done psychotherapy with women as pastors, denominational executives, in academic and administrative roles, and as spouses of clergy to provide worthwhile models and behavioral patterns.

In the *Dictionary of Feminist Theology* (Russell and Clarkson 1996), there is no definition of "pastor" as such. Two entries use the term "pastoral" in ways that seem to reflect the presence of women in that role, but they do not do this definitively. In the entry on pastoral care, Riet Bons-Storm is frustrated by the "shepherd" imagery as male dominant in the Bible. In the entry on pastoral misconduct, Marie M. Fortune mentions only men as perpetrators of sexual misconduct.

Some general reflections from my professional experience, from women's religious literature, and from many informative conversations provide evolving conclusions:

• Women ordained and serving in pastoral roles experience the convergence of personal issues with issues of the professional role in ways quite similar to men's experiences. The role-personhood-personal faith, all-in-one package, engulfs women as surely as it does men.

• Management of marriage and family issues differs from that of men with respect to evening hours, pregnancy, and maternal leave.

• The gender-attraction factor is there for women, but with the well-known gender differences. Seduction, harassment, fantasies, and boundary penalties reflect both realities and prejudices.

- The gender leadership role is painful for many. For gender prejudice, resistance from both women and men, and lessening of role authority is often apparent. Salaries, housing, role responsibilities, upward mobility, and dress codes tend to reflect gender prejudices.

- Support systems indicate significant differences. Denominational and congregational support processes still tend to reflect male needs. Women are often forced to build their own support systems.

- Women's personhood also suffers from the usual 24/7, too many meetings, and unrealistic expectations. As with men, such stress tends toward role confusion, burnout, depression, and sexual misconduct, unless body-mind-spirit health produces appropriate boundaries and nurture.

Sexual Misconduct
by Women Pastors

Before the issues of sexual boundary violations by women pastors can be discussed, I must note significant variations from the violations perpetrated by men. First, the overwhelming majority of victim-survivors are women and girls. Second, sexual abuse by women includes far less physical violence, or the threat of it, than does that perpetrated by men. Third, the statistics and research on women pastors as perpetrators are meager and recent. Yet it is clear that women as pastors also commit professional boundary violations. As with racial issues, it is hard to admit and discuss this issue in the context of church history that has been prejudiced against leadership by women.

The case study of "rape" by a woman pastor presented in chapter 4 indicates that women are capable of sexual misconduct, but typically without the use or threat of physical violence. The emotional intimidation dynamic is present and potent, however. My experience in dealing with women pastors as perpetrators is as limited as the research data, psychotherapeutic experiences, and anecdotal references are. Three cases may nonetheless provide useful reflections.

One case involved a notable woman pastor who was selected over male applicants to become head of staff in a tall-steeple, mainstream congregation. She was immoderately triumphal in telling how she "beat the best" in gaining this appointment. Are there competitive issues here, as occur (but are denied so often) with men?

In another case, a woman head of staff in a smaller congregation was the subject of gossip by her sister pastors about controlling staff members through feminine wiles. She would pick a particular staff member periodically to shower with flirtatious attentions and personal favors, when he pleased her. It seemed to be effective in keeping her staff compliant. Her triumphal stories of how easily she controls her staff are not well-received by women colleagues. Could this be a case of professional seduction?

Another example is a highly competent and ambitious woman pastor who shared in a seduction of her denominational executive. Then, apparently when the pleasure of the relationship and her domination had run its course, she reported this executive for abusing her sexually. He was dismissed. She stayed. The rumors and publicity surrounding this story were so prominent she didn't need to make her point, except to occasionally whisper that she had "brought him down."

Warning Signs
of Clergy Sexual Misconduct

Given the complexities of the clergy role and the numerous possibilities for secrecy and denial, it is sometimes unfair and misleading to list warning signs and characteristics of clergy who engage in sexual abuses. Each situation has its unique factors. We now know so many cases, however, that a few generalities are appropriate and informative.

Here are some general warning signs from clergy involved in or about to perpetrate boundary violations:

- losing the sincere sense of spiritual disciplines (note that simulated religious fervor can mask loss of true spiritual disciplines)
- an undisciplined lifestyle (carelessness in personal life, in handling money, in public life, significant changes in apparel and recreation)
- development of addictions, known or implied, involving food, alcohol/drugs, sleeping, escapist behaviors
- irresponsibility with professional duties (consistently late, missed appointments, incompetent sermon/curriculum preparations, unexplained absences, excessive secrecy, violations of confidentiality)
- eroticized behavior, conversation, and attitude (sexual humor, flirtations, inviting women/men for dinner and church trips alone, bragging about his or her gender attractiveness, use of graphic pornography or cybersex)
- obvious deterioration and negative comments concerning marital relationship

This list is not exhaustive, but it constitutes indicators that can be significant, especially if they represent major changes or come in clusters.

Characteristics of Clergy Sexual Perpetrators

The stories and cases discussed in chapters 4–6 below demonstrate significant characteristics. For a bit of practice in noticing characteristic behavior and attitudes common to various types of abnormal sexual expressions, try to match the following stereotypical comments listed with capital letters, to the abnormal conduct listed with numbers.

RATIONALES	CONDUCT
1. "It's good sex education."	A. Pedophile
2. "It's like having my own little den of iniquity."	(children only)
	B. Incest
3. "Hey, this is fun for everyone."	C. Predator
4. "I can't help myself."	D. Pedophile
5. "I don't see anything wrong with it."	(child or adult)
6. "I just enjoy sex."	E. Rape
7. "Why am I attracted to women's undies?	F. Addict
	G. Cybersex
8. "I got into this deeper than I intended."	H. Paraphilias
9. "I will punish and control."	I. Sexual Harassment

Answers: 1B, 2G, 3C, 4A, 5I, 6F, 7H, 8D, 9E

Therapies and interventions related to cases and stories discussed so far will be presented in chapter 7.

Summary

This chapter focuses on the personhood of the pastor, the unique role a pastor holds in society, the four contemporary maladies that plague pastors, and the applications of what we know about managing clergy sexual misconduct and preventing its occurrence.

The role of pastor is highlighted as a valued spiritual function in human history and as a traditional model for guiding contemporary clergy. However, this role can foster clerical arrogance, the "star factor," and the stress of meeting its exaggerated expectations can contribute to sexual misconduct. A significant prescriptive and growth opportunity for pastors as they manage the clergy role is a personal inventory of the preconscious mental image a pastor has of what is "normal" for this role. Sometimes pastors tyrannize themselves with a role image that exceeds healthy human realities.

How women experience the role of pastor is explored, including examples of how pastors who are women can violate professional boundaries.

The last part of this chapter outlines briefly how we can effectively apply what we are learning about sexual misconduct and its primary preventative, body-mind-spirit health. Warning signs of active or potential sexual misconduct are listed. And a brief quiz is offered to help focus awareness of some attitudes and comments that alert listeners to the warning signals.

Part Two
Cases and Interventions

3.
AN INSTRUCTIVE GENERIC CASE

CASE STUDIES, NARRATIVE, AND STORIES are valuable in human understanding for they tend to open a connection between our thinking and our emotions. This allows us entry into our personal experience in ways rational discussion alone does not provide. The following story has demonstrated its ability to connect cognition and affect in ways important for seeing and understanding the connection between ministry and sexuality as a personal experience, which is often more complex than it appears. Following this story are opportunities to reflect on insights it can provide.

The Pulpits of Madison County

The following story is written as an instructive simulation of the best-selling romantic novel *The Bridges of Madison County* by Robert Waller. That book's enormous popularity parallels the reception of Erich Segal's *Love Story* a generation earlier. Since it deals with sexual passion outside of marriage in a sympathetic manner, a duplication of its format provides a penetrating opportunity to highlight an attitude common to some clergy who have become involved in sexual malfeasance. My book on this subject (see Rediger 1990), has been widely used in clergy circles. Now I use this simulation of the well-known novel as a reminder that it is easy to be seduced into malfeasance by our hormones, our role, and society's permissiveness, even with all the warnings we now have had.

Of course I knew this story was true. I heard it discussed at a clergy meeting in a small Iowa church. But I didn't feel compelled to write about it until two sets of siblings visited me one day and gave me a dog-eared, tear-stained diary. They asked me to write their mother's story in the hope that it would be instructive for pastors and parishioners.

She hated the long, gray winters. Even though the days were short, they seemed to go on forever.

This was another one of those days. The kids had gotten on the bus for school, and Jim was at the office. Now, what to do with this day? The list of things she ought to do was long, the things she wished to do, short. A little excitement and pleasure would do . . . but what?

And then it happened. She heard a car stop in the driveway. Shortly, there was the sound of the doorbell.

She could see that he was tall and slim before she even opened the door. And that smile . . . it burned through her depression. Why did it feel fateful when she placed her hand on the knob to open the door?

It was just another cold call to him. Part of the job, the mission. The more house calls, the more likelihood of another new member. He had been doing this for several weeks now that the bishop had slated the start of the St. Augustine Parish for the first of the year.

Jacob had done this twice before. If things worked out, this would be the third new church he had started here in Madison County. One little congregation was meeting in an unused store in downtown Modos. The second one he had started was further ahead. There the congregation had already bought and was remodeling a former implement dealer's shop on the edge of the little town of Harromog.

He was getting to know Madison County rather well, after nearly four years of this work. His rusting red Camaro was a familiar sight in any town in the county.

As he pulled into the driveway of the well-maintained white and blue house, he readied himself in the usual way. He said a brief prayer, then reached out to the passenger seat for the informational brochure about the new congregation he was starting in Susehpe.

Then he got out of the car and walked up the concrete steps to the front door. Everything seemed the same as on a hundred similar calls . . . except for the slight tingle in the pit of his stomach as he pressed the doorbell button.

He would remember that slight tingle later.

With all her heart she wanted something exciting, something meaningful to happen today. The surge of excitement she felt told her that she was getting what she wanted.

The smile that instantly lighted her dark world was only the beginning. For when she invited him in, he brought energy and command with each step he took. The gloom . . . the aimlessness . . . the searching all ended as he entered and introduced himself more fully.

When she invited him to sit down, he moved with lean confidence to the loveseat and seated himself. He crossed his legs at right angles, the way young men do. And his engaging eyes never left her face as they spoke. He was aware immediately of her female presence.

She nearly collapsed onto the sofa across from him, for her knees were already weak from excitement. But as she felt the firm seat under her, she realized she must get control of her emotions quickly. She crossed her long legs without thinking. Then, seeing the flicker in his eyes, she realized it would be wiser to slide forward and sit on the edge of the seat in a posture she admired in sophisticated women. She, too, never ceased looking into his eyes.

A few moments of silence followed, as each of them regained self-composure. She spoke first, asking if she could make coffee or tea for him. He responded by saying tea would be welcome.

She was feeling more confident now. With a bit of challenge in her voice she asked what kind of tea he preferred. Without hesitation he politely requested Darjeeling. Her confidence betrayed her for a moment as he requested her favorite variety of tea. She loved a man who not only enjoyed tea instead of coffee but knew the kind that satisfied him. That it was her favorite also was unknown to him until she murmured this information.

Intending to be gracious, she started to rise and move toward the kitchen. But it took effort to steady the returned weakness in her knees.

Aplomb was one of her specialties, however. He probably hadn't noticed her internal struggle. So she simply smiled as she walked toward the kitchen, intent on hot water, tea, and pretty china.

He was pleased to be offered tea and then not be disappointed when he asked for Darjeeling. His pleasure continued as she arose gracefully and moved to the kitchen. It was only natural, of course, to gaze at the person who was about to prepare tea. But he was not quite prepared for her sensuous walk. Her wool, plaid culottes were short enough to show curvaceous calves and knees, as the soft wool swished to her stride. What was it that caused her to stop momentarily and turn her head quickly enough to note the movement of his eye from her legs back to her face? She was aware of a coquettish lilt in her voice as she asked whether or not he wished lemon, sugar, or milk with his tea.

Caught off guard by her sudden look and question, he became aware of that tingle again . . . right in the pit of his stomach. He hoped she hadn't noticed how he was looking at her as she turned. With some effort, he made his voice sound calm as he replied that the tea alone was treat enough for drinking.

As if they both realized the danger in their situation, the conversation over tea was platonic. He told her of his new little congregation. And she told him how she, Jim, and the children were looking for a church home. Their shared passion became focused on this new church project. Before he left she had volunteered to serve as his church secretary. She nearly hugged him when he said he would prefer to call her his administrative associate. For his part, he indicated that he would bring material for the church newsletter the following Monday.

Jacob had little trouble preparing his next sermon. His heart was singing with the love he planned to preach about. He tried to keep from thinking about Rachel too much. But it was an inspiration to think of her sitting and listening to this sermon on Sunday.

His euphoria alternated with guilt. He handled the euphoria by telling himself this was normal, healthy eroticism. The guilt subsided when he told himself they would never have sex.

For a couple of days Rachel was dynamite in her tasks. Nothing seemed too hard. She calmed herself when Jim was less enthusiastic about attending this new house church than she was. She didn't mention Jacob or the church to her women friends. Half-consciously she feared their penetrating questions.

The excitement she felt seemed normal and welcome. It was delightful to feel her power to excite a man again. The fact that he was a minister only added to the excitement. Daydreaming of the ministry they were about to share extended her pleasure.

It was the third time they had a long work session together in her home. This had become the most convenient way to handle the new little congregation's administrative work. Here they were uninterrupted by small children, the phone, and a hovering spouse.

It was exciting to work on the bulletin and newsletter together. There were few sick calls to be made in such a small congregation. So after the bulletin and newsletter were completed, their time was spent compiling the data on the information cards he prepared for each house call he made. They laughed together as they read what he wrote about his first call in her home.

The work session automatically included tea time. The preparation of Darjeeling had become a ritual. She would go into the kitchen, put the water on to boil, then assemble the tea, tea cozy, and the delicate china teapot and cups. He would follow her into the kitchen and contribute enthusiastically to her effervescent conversation.

Today his hand casually brushed her buttocks as he walked past her in the kitchen. His favorite vantage spot was the adjacent doorway to a bedroom. Today she playfully sat on his lap for a moment as she arranged the tea service on the coffee table. He felt the tingle again, and she was aware of the weakness in her knees.

It seemed normal for him to invite her to ride along to his monthly visits at the bishop's office. He would drop her off downtown for shopping, or in the park, if it was a nice day. After the bishop came more happy time, the name they gave to their nonworking time together. Lunch at a coffee shop, or a picnic in the park, or whatever.

The regional meeting of pastors who were starting new churches provided a longed-for opportunity. She accompanied him, of course, and he enjoyed introducing her as his "right arm of ministry." The sessions concluded about nine, after a shared meal in the dining hall of the host church. They were the last to leave, watching other pastors hurry to their cars for the long drives home.

When he turned the key in the ignition of his faithful Camaro, they heard only a brief grinding, then a click and silence. There was still an attendant at the corner gas station, but he told them the mechanic couldn't work on the car until morning.

Exchanged glances, phone calls to spouses, and a short walk to a motel. Here they were, unlocking doors to adjacent rooms.

It seemed so natural to look over each other's room, and then decide which one to share. Showering was the delicious discovery of each other's body. The long, quiet night was the throbbing indulgence of exquisite passion. And their shared devotions in the morning seemed to bring God right into their room.

Heads sometimes turned as they came out of a restaurant or movie theatre together. For it was not only the old, red Camaro that was becoming familiar in town. But their euphoria was often sullied now by forced explanations to spouses, and by worry about the turning heads in town. But things were going very well in the new congregation. Their energy was an inducement to ministry for others, even as it was seductive for Jacob and Rachel.

But it was those waking times in the night that were most tormenting. Each of them lying beside a sleeping spouse toward whom they felt no attraction produced yearning for the forbidden. How long could they protect their passion? Was divorce realistic? Would it ever be possible to return to their former lives?

There was lead in his stomach instead of the familiar tingle, as he tapped at her door this morning. Her face was tear-strained as she silently let him in for what they both knew was the last time.

The appointment with the bishop was quick and painless, however. Jacob agreed that the established church in Arkansas was a good appointment for all concerned. Farewell services are never easy. Some parishioners were lavish with praise and best wishes. Several deacons and veteran members were cool in their goodbyes. The two spouses didn't attend.

Rachel wondered if he ever got her last note, which was inside the carton of Darjeeling tea she left in his mailbox. Jacob wondered if she ever found the note he had slipped inside the china teapot.

As she tried to bring her life back under control, she wondered if he thought of her, and how he thought of her. Tea time each morning was a bittersweet experience. This was the time she now spent scrawling rambling, tearful entries in her diary. Often she frightened herself by wondering what her children would think someday when they discovered the book of her secret.

Pastoral duties filled his days now, except for morning tea time. This was his time to work on the book he was writing about the love stories of the Bible. Memorable pleasures with Rachel flashed through his mind often as he wrote. Invariably he remembered how she so tenderly called him "my own man of God." Occasionally he remembered that Cindy in Modos and Barb in Harromog also used to refer to him fondly in this way.

This story and its characters are fictional. In a generalized way, however, this is a story I have heard from the lips of more than one clergyperson. Caveat emptor!

Analysis of the Story

This story is used here as a generic case study because it contains the elements of a contextual clergy sexual ethic and misconduct common to the pastoral role as well as being common in other helping professions as well as human experience. It demonstrates how a chance meeting with mutual seduction and synergistic passion can be so common, natural, and welcome, yet have such disastrous consequences.

As an exercise in understanding the dynamics of this common scenario for clergy sexual misconduct, please reread the story and then respond to the following items:

1. List the steps you can imagine led to the initial meeting of Jacob and Rachel.

2. Describe the steps in the initial seduction that occurred in Rachel's home.

3. Who had the most control of the developing liaison? Why is this true?

4. Who was responsible for setting appropriate professional boundaries? Why?

5. What mistakes did Jacob make in the initial meeting with Rachel?

6. What should he have done instead of the mistake?

7. What was wrong with this "natural" love affair?

8. Critique the behavior of each participant in this story:
   —Jacob
   —Rachel
   —Jim
   —Bishop
   —Congregants
   —Conveners of the clergy gatherings

9. What spiritual-mental-physical disciplines could Jacob have developed that would have prevented this boundary violation?

10. Describe a possible alternative scenario if Jacob had established appropriate professional boundaries.

11. What do you believe is the common opinion of congregants regarding what is called "adultery," "an affair," "cheating," "illicit sex"?

12. What do you believe is the common opinion of congregants regarding sex outside of marriage when it involves their pastor in comparison with their own sexual behavior. Discuss such differences.

13. What steps would you have taken and recommended if the bishop had asked you to be a consultant in handling this case?

Both the obvious and the subtle dynamics of this story of clergy sexual misconduct are important. Which of the following elements did you notice, and which escaped your attention?

- the effect of being unprepared to deal with sexual attraction
- the effects of testosterone and estrogen
- the synergy of shared spiritual-sexual euphoria
- the effects of boredom and mild depression

- the influence of the setting in which mutual attraction occurs
- the influence of the time of day
- the cues of attraction Jacob and Rachel exhibited
- the relationship between spirituality and sexuality.

List other elements you believe contributed to the mutual seduction:
1.
2.
3.

Now apply your insights to how this situation would change if Jacob and Rachel had begun as a pastor-parishioner in a counseling relationship.

This case is presented to demonstrate the most common professional boundary violation that occurs in organized religion. The common factor is a pastor-parishioner working together in ministry programs, or in a pastor-parishioner counseling relationship, as a man and a woman with normal libido. This generic case shows how normal it can be for two sexual human beings who are together on a regular basis to become attracted to each other. Then come choices as to whether to proceed to an eroticized relationship.

Traditional theology and pastoral practice does not allow for sexual behavior and abuse in such relationships. It has long been assumed that pastors would know better than to cross the boundary of both nonmarital sex and professional ethics. We are learning that such boundaries must be mandated more clearly and forcefully.

In a counseling situation, involving a pastor and parishioner, one has a position of caring authority and skill. The other comes in search of competent and safe counseling. The sexual attraction may be equal or a magnetic polarity of reciprocal needs. We now know that the counselee is in a position of vulnerability in such a relationship, while the clergyperson is at-risk in the temptation to take advantage of the parishioner's vulnerability.

Clergy and other helping professionals are learning that professional boundaries must be set and observed. Sexual passions that seem so normal can quickly sabotage the helper-helpee interaction that is needed. The best control process occurs when both counselee and counselor observe the professional boundary. But that is often unrealistic, given the needs of the counselee. The primary responsibility for maintaining this boundary must rest with the clergyperson. We hope that further support and enforcement will come from the congregation and denominational offices. Understanding professional boundaries must begin in seminary training and models.

Summary

A generic case is presented, modeled after a best-selling novel about adult sex outside of marriage told in a romantic, sympathetic way. Here the story is translated into a normal clergy setting in order to show that the romantic illusions of mutual attraction can create a serious pitfall for pastors who are unprepared to handle such common situations. The story demonstrates how sincere spiritual ministry is not immune from the passions of lonely women and wandering pastors. A reminder that the pastor-parishioner counseling situation is a frequent and parallel setting for healthy or abusive behavior follows the story of a pastor-parishioner ministry relationship. Such situations represent a high statistical area of boundary violations.

This case illustrates one common scenario of boundary violations. Mutual attraction is a sensitive issue because it reminds us that responsibility for mutual seduction lies with both parties, plus other persons in related relationships. It illustrates how natural sexual needs and attractions are. And it shows that primary responsibility for stopping attractions and seductions must rest with the professional clergyperson. For he or she is attractive because of the professional role, is most knowledgeable about intimacy and the consequences of sexual misconduct, and is most able to help to see that the needs of the other party are met through appropriate resources. Yet the complications of such situations require training that many pastors do not have. Studying and discussing this case can lead to better skills for managing at-risk ministry situations and personal sexuality.

Analysis and discussion questions are offered to aid in applying such common clergy misconduct to personal experience.

This is the first of a variety of clergy sexual misconduct and sexual disorders cases that are presented in this book.

4.
WORST-CASE SCENARIOS: CHILD ABUSE

If any of you put a stumbling block before one of these little ones who believe in me, it would be better for you if a great millstone were hung around your neck and you were thrown into the sea.

—MARK 9:42

MOLESTATION OF CHILDREN and predation of adults is more than men behaving badly. It is heinous. It is evil. We must express this revulsion and anger in order to clear our minds and hearts for understanding sexual abuse, and then work for solutions.

Even when we know that pedophilia is a possible outcome of personality disorder, mental impairment, and being abused as a child, it is difficult to be merciful and understanding with those who abuse children sexually. Yet for Christians and Jews there is a mandate to take time to understand offenders and abusers of all kinds, to care for and protect victims, and to pursue healing, justice, and healthful relationships. So we begin our review of clergy sexual misconduct with the worst possible scenario, and then seek to understand and to facilitate care and justice.

Pedophilia is the erotic attraction of an adult to prepubescent children and the use of children for sexual gratification and demonstration of a capacity to dominate. This is a simple definition that can serve as a starting point. More thorough definitions are also helpful, but the literature on the sexual abuse of children by adults contains a variety of medical, psychological, legal, and sometimes contradictory definitions. Therefore a simple, clear, and thorough definition seems unlikely. This does not mean, however, that we cannot find understandings that will inform and guide us. This chapter summarizes significant information.

A preliminary note: except for the terms pedophile and ephebophile, which refer to a nearly exclusive sexual abuse pattern, in this book I use the term abuser to include all forms of sexual abuse, including violence, and the term molester to include those who touch, talk to, and relate to children in inappropriate ways.

Sexual abuse of children is much more common than we had thought. The incidence is too high, not only among Catholic priests but also among Protestant clergy (about 2–3 percent are offenders). The massive data on pedophiles and molesters indicates that each perpetrator has multiple victims. Current data indicate that offenders are almost exclusively adult males. Boys are victimized five times as often as girls.

The world of the pedophile, molester, and abuser of children is shadowy or unknown to many. Nearly everyone knows that many children are abused, yet the realities and proportions need to be factored into our consciousness lest we simply overreact, or wring our hands and walk away. In this chapter I summarize information that will aid in understanding this global but very personal phenomenon.

The general statistics about sexual abuse of children indicate that approximately 13 percent of those abused were abused by strangers. Nearly 28 percent were abused by friends. Baby-sitters committed approximately 3 percent of such abuses. About 57 percent were abused by family members—21 percent by natural fathers, 12 percent by stepfathers, 10 percent by brothers, 10 percent by uncles, 5 percent by grandfathers, and 19 percent of the abuses were committed by close family friends. The type of molestation varies, with 23 percent of convicted molesters having committed rape, 24 percent statutory rape, 33 percent indecent liberties, 3 percent indecent exposure, 6 percent incest, along with indecent liberties and contributing to the delinquency of a minor, etc. (statistics from Van Dam 2001).

Although figures vary in the research reports, it is apparent that about 25 percent of abusers were abused themselves as children. The typical offender often reports feeling "different" as a child and may have adopted mannerisms that either express or hide that feeling. Often abusers of children regress to childlike behavior when they are with children and report enjoying this deeply. Pedophiles target children almost exclusively. It is not uncommon for other sex offenders to victimize both children and adults. Offenders often have a history of precocious sexual fantasizing and frequently augment current fantasies with substance abuse. They tend to rationalize and minimize their behavior and its consequences. And since they seldom have appropriate sex partners, recidivism is predictable when there is no effective therapy and supervision.

A Friend of Boys

A suave, handsome male pastor in his mid-fifties came into my office, introduced himself in an affable and articulate manner, and fell silent. When he began to speak again, it took him a while to get to the point. I heard about a "deep, dark secret" and about how frightened he was that its revelation would ruin his job, his marriage, his reputation. Then it came out. This pastor had recently been followed by the parent of a young boy whom he was driving from a Cub Scout meeting. If he had not noticed the father in his rearview mirror, the pastor would have taken the boy from the meeting to the local Dairy Queen for a treat, and from there to the park for oral sex. Finishing his story, the pastor looked like a man who had been rescued from certain death. "Thank God," he whispered. "Thank God I saw the car." He was to repeat this phrase often during our sessions.

He seemed somewhat relieved to have said it out loud and to have assured himself that he had not been caught. He spent the rest of the hour telling me about several young boys with whom he had had sex in parishes he had served. There seemed to be some remorse, and there were brief expressions of shame and guilt; but mostly he expressed relief to be talking about it. At the end of the appointment he quickly pulled himself together and walked out of the office with aplomb.

The next appointment was spent on life and generational history. He believed his father was gay and oriented to little boys, but he had never seen any evidence. He had had a couple of sexual experiences with an uncle when he visited his farm one summer. He recalled these experiences with little demonstration of feeling. Toward the end of the hour he began telling me about a favorite pastor when he was in upper grades and junior high school. The next appointment he told me more. He obviously enjoyed the memories of his relationship with this man, which included oral and anal sex.

He had done well in school and gone right through college and seminary with singleness of purpose, as if he could hardly wait to be a pastor. He had married a college girlfriend who was intent on a career in nursing. They had two children but little sexual intimacy. He had never molested his son and was not even tempted to do so, he said. But young boys in church were a constant attraction, and several became his victims. His wife seemed to suspect him and warned him once that if he ever got into sexual trouble, she would leave with the children immediately. She seemed content to concentrate on her successful career and the children, yet she often joined him to appear at church events where both were expected.

There was a significant pattern in this pastor's relationship with boys. He spent lots of time building a friendly, trusting relationship with each boy before having sex. He even reported that each

of the boys loved him dearly and engaged in sex willingly. None
had ever reported him to parents or authorities; he did not seem
worried that they would! It was not until he was followed by a
boy's father that fear seized him and caused him to seek help.

Counseling this pastor posed significant problems, both for him
and for me. The now-standard law requiring the reporting of
abuse of children had not been passed. But after we found ways
for him to realize the enormity of his abuse of these boys, and he
had established a measure of self-control, we discussed the strategy for aiding in the recovery of boys he had abused.

We found that the boys in previous parishes were grown, and
all seemed to be functioning normally, except for one who had
been in and out of jail and therapy for several years. It took several months for the pastor to make discreet inquiries to gather this
information. There had been two victims in this present parish.
With one boy there had been no sex, only a growing relationship.
He agreed to work toward getting this boy to transfer his church
relationship to another responsible youth adviser. This left us with
one boy to get into therapy, and it was the boy whose father had
tailed the pastor. The pastor discovered that this boy's father had
some psychological problems, with a characteristic paranoia. The
boy had been physically abused at home and had a poor record in
school. There was a good mental health center in the town, and
the boy and his whole family were established in counseling there
by the time this pastor resigned to take another church.

Before he moved, I insisted that he establish a relationship with
a mental health professional in his new location, as well as the
controls on his behavior we had prescribed. His wife finally joined
us and readily agreed to assist him in watching for signs of weakness and a recurrence of the abuse. They both agreed to work on
the intimacies of their relationship with a sex therapist, and with
personal reading and study. I asked him if he wanted anything further from me. He said he wanted me to be ready to tell his whole
story to his denominational executive if his wife contacted me and

told of any recurrence. I told him that I would talk over possibilities if such an occasion occurred.

We reviewed again the seriousness of the sexual abuses he had committed. I discussed his options again, from going to each boy and family and confessing and doing what he could to repair the damage, to assisting through anonymous prayers, to letting the situations alone and doing all he could to help his congregation and denomination deal with such abuses.

A clinical and spiritual syndrome are apparent in this case of pedophilia. The arrogance, clever manipulations, lack of empathy, denial/illusions, the excitement of risking illicit encounters over and over, and self-centeredness demonstrate a narcissistic personality disorder. This pastor did not have all the fully developed characteristics of a narcissistic personality disorder, but we reviewed these together to aid him in understanding himself. Narcissistic disorders are fascinating to work with therapeutically, but hell to live with. The pastor in this case had enough insight and enough built-in controls to serve as a foundation for a more disciplined lifestyle.

It is disturbing to note the professional and spiritual dynamics in this common story. This pastor's professional competence was outstanding. He was socially skilled, above average in intelligence, and effective in parish leadership. Yet it was apparent that professional competence was often used in service to his libido. His spirituality was similarly contaminated. For his intimate relationships were mostly a façade. And his religious faith was compartmentalized, along with a theology that supported his denial.

Another Version

Another version of this story is evident in the media photos, the chronological development and the clinical research that point to another common syndrome. This has been demonstrated to me in the stories I have heard from several bishops and priests, including an exorcist. They tell of priests who are abject and confused, able to function only at a minimal level of professional competence, though they may look normal to parishioners. The lives of such priests revolve around the temporary gratification of sexual encounters with children, usually boys, and the plotting and imaginations of such encounters. They are often mortified by their behavior, dismayed at the prospect of discovery, and confused by their own distorted sexual drives and behavior.

A clinical and spiritual syndrome is apparent in such cases as well as in the previously presented case. The distracted or vacant look in their eyes, a hesitant or confused self-presentation, the depressed, though occasionally explosive demeanor, a submissive or servile attitude in relationships, and the evasive, conflicting responses to queries fit the depressive, paranoid, borderline personality disorders. Though they may have a few casual adult friends—and dozens of sexual contacts with boys—they often live and function as loners. According to research and treatment reported by Father Steven Rossetti, Ph.D., Director of the St. Luke Institute in Silver Spring, Maryland, the neuropsychological impairment in pedophiles and ephebophiles tested with standard brain impairment tests reveals about one-half of them have diminished rational capacities. This may help account for their deviant, ungovernable behavior, and record of recidivism. Photos and TV news clips of Father William Porter, infamous for scores of sexual abuses in three parishes, seem to show the face and presence of this syndrome. Besides the clinical characteristics, such clergy manifest another distorted version of the clergy role and spirituality. Serving as a pastor, rabbi, or priest when constantly distracted by sexual urges and fantasies, patently diverts attention, energy, and time from ministry. And a theology that can include such monstrous behavior and such consequent guilt trips is distorted indeed.

Variations in both of these major syndromes exist, of course. And unless an observer is trained or alert to see and understand such characteristics, this pastor and this priest could be—and have been—seen as relatively normal variants of clergy types. Ninety-five percent of child molesters are known and trusted as familiar members of society (Van Dam 2001). At least one of the benefits of the increasing exposure of such cases is that many more of the leaders and the faithful in organized religion are becoming mindful and wary of such personal characteristics. Spiritual leaders have a responsibility to guide and enhance such new awareness.

Pedophilia is distinguished by some authorities from ephebophilia, which is sexual attraction to and abuse of pubescent youths. Research has not yet clarified all the distinguishing characteristics of these disorders. Pedophilia, however, appears to focus on young boys who, because of their innocence, can be treated as objects—as if they were young dolls to be toyed with, manipulated, and examined—for the abuser's pleasure. Undeveloped physical characteristics apparently allow abusers to fantasize about their own innocence and satyrize compliant bodies. The abusers seem as intent upon active and adoring relationships with boys as upon the sexual behavior. The abuser pretends that his victim participates for mutual gratification, and he wants to act as if this were a healthy relationship. The abuser will often take a boy under his wing and act as a mentor. Such boys perceive a lack of affection and support from their parents and find a replacement in an affectionate adult male, who often seduces them but who gives them enduring attention and support. Not all boys yield willingly to either the pedophile or the ephebophile. But such abusive men seem to have a talent for finding boys who will be responsive and for grooming them for sexual encounters. When these characteristics are understood, it is not hard to see the reason that therapy with such men and their victims is so difficult. It should also help us recognize that such men, even after extensive therapy, should never be allowed to have private and authority-figure relationships with young boys again. (For a review of coerced sexual relationships in schools for adolescent boys, see Rosetti 1996.)

Pedophilia (the term usually used in popular discussion of both forms of abuse) is a topic much in the news these days, partly because we sense that it can have terrible consequences for young victims. Distorted self-image, confused sexual identity, inability to form healthy relationships, distrust of authority figures, becoming a sexually abusive adult—any or all of these are likely consequences of abuse. The suicide rate among victims of abuse is unusually high. The wonder, perhaps, is that many victims somehow manage to develop rather normally and live relatively happy lives. For all, however, there is a deep, dark secret inside them, potentially able to distort their lives and relationships significantly.

The causes of pedophilia and ephebophilia are not clear, although genetic factors and early childhood experiences—including abuse—seem to be involved. These perpetrators are disproportionately male, more frequently heterosexual in cases of ephebophilia, more homosexual in cases of pedophilia.

Intervention is clearly required. For it is clear is that many children are sexually abused, and clergy are involved far more often than we had suspected. We should be alert to danger signals and take responsible action when we see them. The signals include obviously strange patterns of behavior by an adult playing with children, and reports or body language in which children hint at their discomfort in the presence of that adult. Other signals include singling out one (or more) boys for loving attention, unwelcome touching, gift giving, shared "secrets," too much time together alone, and denial that these are inappropriate relationships. Some of these behaviors can be accidental and are not necessarily indicators by themselves. But in clusters they often indicate an inappropriate relationship or abuse. The observation of such signals should be verified, ideally by discussing them first with the child and then, if indicated, with the clergyperson. If this is impossible for any reason, including the observer's hesitance to approach the matter, someone in a position to help must be notified, and then monitored to see that caring, remedial action is taken.

One more variation on this anguished subject of the sexual abuse of children needs to be considered: incest. Even the word brings a swirl of emotions to healthy persons!

A Dad and His Daughters

"He kept excusing his sexual advances toward our daughters by calling them 'sex education.' He would say things like, 'You should be happy that I'm willing to teach my daughters about sex'; or, 'Don't be so prudish. I have to help them be sexually liberated for the kind of world they're growing up in.' I knew something was wrong, but I felt too hurt, too afraid, too angry to do anything about it."

These are the words of a midlife pastor's wife. For several visits she recited, in a numb monotone, the random details and chronology of this pastor's sexual abuse of their daughters. It was not until the fourth appointment that she was able to break down and sob out some of the excruciating emotions she had been feeling for a couple of years. Then we had a chance to open up the whole pattern of his sexual manipulations and his abuse of these daughters.

She first became aware of the problem in her family when she noticed the long, silent periods while her husband was in the bathroom giving each girl her nightly bath before he put her to bed. Her uneasiness turned to anxious concern as she asked her husband if he ever had erotic feelings about his daughters, and why he made such passionate love to her on Thursday and Sunday nights, the nights that he bathed their daughters. His irritable response did not seem appropriate.

One evening she stopped outside the closed bathroom door and heard the daughter, inside with her husband, say something like, "Ouch, Daddy, that hurts!" She pushed the door open and saw her husband sexually fondling the girl. Though she was stunned, she made a calm remark about bedtime and left the bathroom. Later that night, when she and her husband were in bed, she asked about the bathroom episode. That was when he began his remarks about his sexual behavior with the girls being good sex education. She felt intense surges of anger, hurt, fear, and confusion.

Then came revulsion. One day she watched a television talk show about sexual abuse. As she heard the stories of several women who had been abused by their fathers while growing up, and as she learned about the emotional distortions this caused in their lives, a feeling of revulsion came over her so strongly that she lost her breakfast. After the revulsion came anger—anger mixed with guilt.

This was the turning point. That night the woman confronted her husband with the fury of an enraged parent. When he tried his usual excuses, she escalated to accusations and ultimatums. When he did not respond, she threatened to go to his bishop with the story. The she stormed out of their bedroom and spent a sleepless night in the spare bedroom.

The next morning her husband warned her not to tell the bishop or anyone else, because this would only lead to disaster for all of them. She spent her day in emotional turmoil. When her husband returned from his church meeting that night, she told him that either he must go with her to my office or she would take the risk of telling the bishop. He shocked her by saying, "Go ahead and tell him, and see what it gets us!" That was when she knew she was in a double bind. She could not tell the bishop, and she could not let the abuse continue. The next morning she phoned my office and scheduled an appointment.

The most difficult part of the process was strategizing. The woman felt trapped, and her emotions of rage, hurt, and confusion were turning inward. This created a block to planning effective action. Over and over she repeated, "I'm not sure what to do."

In her appointments she now began to consider a word I used several times in reflecting her thinking back to her. The word was "permission." I said, "It sounds as if you need permission to act on one of your strategies." She did not accept this idea at first. But then she reflected that she was already taking action—she was holding the feelings and energy inside. It took several appointments to sort out these feelings and memories and to contemplate the possible strategies.

There was a look of determination on her face as she arrived for our appointment one day. She announced immediately that she had decided to go to the bishop with her story. Then she immediately stared at my face and became silent. I said nothing. After a long silence, she asked, "Well? Well, what do you think?" After another long silence, she sobbed. After regaining her composure, she said, "It's very hard, you know." I nodded and remained silent. "I am outraged by his behavior. I'm suffering with my daughters. And I'm afraid of what will happen to them as they grow up. And now I'm considering taking action that will probably result in our disgrace and my husband's leaving the ministry. And, oh, by the way, I will never let my husband bathe our daughters again!"

She didn't cry now; she just stared at me. I said, "Wouldn't it be nice if someone would do this for you and guarantee that everything would turn out beautifully?" She smiled feebly and remained silent for a while. Then she said, "I'm going to do it—alone if I have to. I know that I'm not alone, but I sure feel alone." At the close of this appointment I asked her to bring a written statement next time that would indicate clearly her chosen plan of action. She left with a very troubled look on her face.

At the beginning of the next appointment, she immediately took a typed statement out of her purse, read it to me, and then stared at it silently. She tried to hand it to me, but I asked her to date it and sign it. She did so very slowly. Then I said, "Who are the witnesses to this signature?" She stared off into space, and then slowly said, "You, my daughters, God, my mother, my father, my friends Sylvia and Marcie. I guess everyone in the whole world will soon be my witnesses!" I said, "Is your husband a witness to your signature on this statement?" "Yes," she said emphatically. I asked, "Do you think he would join you here or with some other counselor if you showed him this paper?" "I don't know," she said. "It's worth a try, isn't it?" "Let's set another appointment for you, and in the meantime you decide whether or not you will show him this paper, and whether or not you can accept him as a partner in handling this matter."

She came to the next appointment with a tired face. She said she had shown the paper to her husband and he had been furious. After he calmed down, he agreed to come for an appointment.

He is now a consultant in computer programming. She is recertified to teach. The girls are doing better in school.

Commentary

In the DSM-IV (the diagnostic and statistical manual of the American Psychiatric Association [APA] 1994), incest is included under pedophilia: "Individuals may limit their activities to their own children, stepchildren, or relatives, or may victimize children outside their families." This then requires a diagnosis of exclusive type (chronic, fixated, or pedophile), or nonexclusive type (regressed, episodic, or incest offender). Such classifications are disputed by some researchers with studies that show many such offenders engage in a variety of sexual molestations with children, within or outside the family (Van Dam 2001).

Offenders typically have excuses and defenses for their abuses, which indicates that their behavior has a cognitive component often missing in exclusive pedophiles. They pretend a sex education intent, blame their spouse for not giving them satisfying sex, plead job stress, or call the abuses a mistake. In truth, such rationalizations are strong indicators of their proclivities and willingness to violate boundaries. In my pastoral counseling experience I have noted the "temporary offender," who molests a child during the opportunities of childhood, then reverts to other unhealthy modes or develops a more mature lifestyle. Then there is the "lifelong" offender whose chronic patterns fit the DSM-IV exclusive type.

We should note again the growing evidence of female participation in child sexual abuse. Women now initiate sexual abuse of children just as they may initiate abuses of adults, though recent studies indicate that many participate as willing or unwilling partners of male offenders.

The effects on victim-survivors of incest tend to follow the grievous patterns of maladies suffered by those sexually abused in childhood, as cited above. There do seem to be several that may be specific to incest. Prostitution and eating disorders have been noted. For all victims (those who never recover) and survivors (those who achieve relatively healthy sexuality), however, there is always the "deep, dark secret" with its haunting memories (see Knauer 2002). Evidence and charges of incest, as with pedophilia and molestation, require prompt and dedicated proscriptive action. Along with supportive and caring therapy for victim-survivors, offenders should by directed into therapy groups and/or family therapy.

Intervention and Therapy

There are risks in all this—the risk of allegations against the innocent, of witch hunts, and of a breakdown in the traditional trust of clergy. On their part, innocent clergy might find it difficult now to relax and act naturally with children. It is essential, therefore, that people be sensitive and objective as they move from one stage to another in the process of discovery. But the risk must be taken, and clergy must learn to accept uncomfortable inquiries as evidence of human concern.

Psychotherapy and perhaps medical treatment are necessary. Verification of pedophilia or ephebophilia demands immediate separation of the offender from all victims—actual or potential. There can be no question of moving a pastor to another church where the same kind of situation will arise. Treatment of the disorder includes intensive therapy and carefully restricted vocational and leisure activities. Recidivism is high; continued monitoring of the offender is necessary. Clergy who suffer from this terrible distortion of sexuality can live productive lives, but there can be no thought of things getting back to normal.

Molesters may or may not need such stringent interventions and therapies. With credible allegations, however, there should be immediate separation from possible victims, until a professional assessment is made. If the molestation is sporadic, and intertwined with addictions and personal childhood abuse, stringent therapy is needed, either through the addiction model (more later) or more conventional therapies.

Incest offenders, since they tend to have a greater cognitive component in their behavior, may often participate appropriately in their own assessment and plan of therapy, though a professional must be in charge.

The victims of abuse by clergy must be given special attention. Children have come to church and then been violated. The church in which this has happened cannot waste energy attempting to save face or telling itself that it cannot have happened here. It did. Now the challenge is to be available to the victims, with all the compassion and competent help that they need. Occasionally now some streetwise youths are able to use clergy vulnerability and public outrage with child abuse for their own sinister purposes. But accusations and danger signals must always be taken seriously, because they typically indicate abuse.

Summary

Three versions of the persistent sexual abuse of children are presented, all three by clergy.

The normal reaction of healthy adults is shock and abhorrence when they hear of the sexual abuse of children. The shock factor increases when the abuser is clergy, for this is not only misconduct, it is malfeasance. Abuse by clergy not only violates a person's civil rights but breaks the trust children should be able to have in pastors, and it breaks faith with the vows of ordination. The human capacity for ignoring or becoming accustomed to the shock of child sexual abuse is augmented by our embarrassment in talking about sexuality in any form, except for pornographic comedians or bar humor. Further, the constant efforts of abusers to cover abuse with secrecy and the fear of many of getting involved with police or lawyers prevent the American public and the church or synagogue from knowing the prevalence of child sexual abuse and the long-term consequences of childhood abuse on the victim and society and on the church. Consequently, we who are committed to religious faith and its institutions must not only be vigilant regarding this nightmarish experience for children and those who love them, but we must be willing to oppose casual attitudes regarding this trivialization of sexuality and press to uncover the sexual abuse of children wherever we see warning signals. For the warning signals must be heeded not only because they likely point to abuse but because they in themselves indicate unhealthy sexuality.

Intervention and therapy need more attention in organized religion. Codes of conduct have been written and are being revised in mainstream Protestant denominations. The Committee on Ethics of the Central Conference of American Rabbis is refining its applications of the Code of Ethics for interventions and therapy. Ethnic denominations struggle with strong traditions as they work on American versions of intervention and therapy. Religious leaders who are women are developing gender specific support and thera-pies. And all denominations are working to improve care for vic-tim-survivors, therapy and support for deposed clergy, assisting congregations in recovery and prevention, and in finding ways to pay for these costly and necessary ministries. Our efforts are laud-able, yet our sexual disarray remains largely unresolved.

5. INSIDIOUS SEXUAL MISCONDUCT

IN THIS CHAPTER I move into a less onerous area of distorted sexuality, but it is on the same sexual-spiritual continuum as the sexual abuse of children typologies treated in chapter 4. The continuum suggested here is similar to the one offered by Marie Fortune in her workshop manual, *Clergy Sexual Misconduct* (1997). She posits two extremes: at one end is the "wanderer," an offender who doesn't understand boundaries and whose offenses are not likely to be abusive. At the other extreme is the "predator," who is an intentional, chronic offender and is likely to violate and abuse. She emphasizes that the effects on victims are not determined by the type of offender. The continuum used in this book arranges offenders in clusters determined by mental impairment and chronic victimization (chapter 4), personality disorders and habitual moral violations (chapter 5), dalliance, opportunism, and naïveté (chapter 3), and poor socialization, low frustration threshold, genetic defect, and inappropriate models (chapter 6).

Gary Schoener, a leading researcher in sexual misconduct by professionals in the helping disciplines and director of the Walk-in Counseling Center, Minneapolis, posits six categories (0–5) of offenders: category 0 he identifies as "persons who have little or no knowledge of professional standards"; category 1 identifies professionals who are "mildly neurotic" and remorseful; category 2 identifies professionals who are "neurotic/isolated," with significant emotional difficulties; category 3 identifies professionals with "compulsive character disorders," who engage in repetitive, compulsive sexual acting out; category 4 identifies professionals with "sociopathic and narcissistic character disorders," who exploit others without true guilt or remorse; category 5 identifies professionals with "psychotic or borderline personalities," who suffer from long-term serious emotional disturbance. Schoener offers a prognosis in which categories 3, 4, and 5 can rarely be rehabilitated. With category 2 the prognosis is variable, depending often on duration of victimization. Those in category 1 typically have a single sexual involvement, without evidence of general boundary violations with clients, and will likely regain control through remorse and self-discipline. The looser clustering schema offered here, as indicated in the chapters on offenders, allows for more variables and mixed intensities. Again, Marie Fortune's admonition that these typologies are about offenders rather than victims should be noted with these three classification systems. The new understandings of victim-survivors will be discussed later.

Some researchers and writers have offered distinct definitions and classifications for sexual offenders and their offenses. Most recognize the diversities and blurred distinctions in such classification systems, but offer them for whatever value they contribute to understanding and working with the realities of sexual misconduct. John Ratey and Catherine Johnson, in their book *Shadow Syndromes* (1997), offer valuable insights regarding the realities of blurred categories and uneven characteristics of clinical diagnosis. They show how discrete classifications based on symptoms is misleading. Instead, we need biological and behavioral histories in order to understand likely behaviors and helpful therapies. My research and experience agree with this perception of diversity and individual variations. I simply offer three groupings, based on seriousness of impairment and consequences and on typical patterns of behavior. These chapters on clergy sexual misconduct indicate such groupings.

The previous chapter grouped together pedophile, molester, and incest offender primarily because they focus on young children, even though they may include youth and adults in their travesties of appropriate human sexual behavior. The predator and sex addict seem related in the insidious nature of their thought processes and behavior and in the chronic need for and selection (inadvertent or intentional) of their victims.

Typically, there is less repugnance directed to predators than to pedophiles—unless you are a victim. In fact, there is even some admiration and jealousy, often secretive, associated with a playboy/playgirl, stud/babe. This is not so with the dark side of predation—the stalker, rapist, brutalizer/batterer. I use the term predator to include both aspects. For intentional targeting of victims is common to both, while the method of entrapment varies. The seductive predator seeks victims who will respond to enticement, while the rapist is coercive.

Since "predator" is not the most common term applied to aggressive-violent offenders, a definition relevant to this material is in order. "Predator," as used here, denotes a person who aggressively, seductively, or coercively exploits another for sexual gratification, dominance, and related motivations.

Predators exist among clergy and officials of organized religion. We are still learning that this is a pervasive scandal. Media and the legal system have helped penetrate the mystique of ordination and the secrecy of hierarchical governance. Although clergy bashing is common in the media, there is also a deprecating style of reporting on other authority figures. The intent is often sincere or dutiful, but contemporary media must use shock and drama to engage public attention in an over-stimulated society.

In the earlier wave of clergy sex scandals, pastors, priests, and rabbis were the focus of attention. For it was still assumed that denominational and institutional officials were without blame and would correct scandalous situations when they were pointed out. In the current media reporting and general consciousness, the scandals are shown to involve all levels of organized religion. The following cases are indications of this pervasive moral culpability and misconduct.

The Wanton Seminary Professor

He seemed to be always smiling, jocular, and friendly to everyone, but there was also a sense of wariness and distance. He was not close to any faculty members, though he hung out with a couple of them who were rumored to be having affairs. He spent more time with women than with men. His attentions focused on attractive, vivacious women, with whom he seemed to have an animal magnetism. Frequently he was seen with his arm around a woman's shoulders or waist as he talked to them. And his amorous attentions often included taking such women out for lunch or a drink, to run their errands, or to destinations unknown.

His wife held a prestigious position in the seminary's administration. She was competent, respected, and devoted to her home, which she kept immaculate, and where she pursued her hobbies of knitting, bird-watching, and painting. She was not seen often at social events, and when present at seminary functions, she was quiet, friendly, and typically beside her husband.

This professor generated a sexual mystique with his attentions to women. He owned a luxury, full-sized camper van, which was a focus of campus rumors. Students irreverently called it the "passion wagon." There were titillating rumors, and also some concern and anger among students concerned with the morality and ethics of the seminary. Several of them met and devised a letter to the dean of the faculty, a kindly, well-known scholar whose age and competence made him a respected figure. In this letter these students listed "boundary violations," which was a new term then. They told of sexual humor, the notorious van, and suspected amorous dalliances. And a major complaint was that this professor's class lectures and assigned study projects were far below academic standards.

No one ever officially heard of the disposition of this letter. Rumor had it that the dean organized an investigative unit that suggested the seminary president reprimand this professor, and that the professor be urged to be more morally circumspect. The president, who was rumored to be having an affair, did nothing publicly. And the dean apparently was content to admonish the professor. Discontented students began to realize the futility of their complaints when it was announced that a new chapel being built at the seminary would be named for this professor, whose generous gift had made it possible.

The professor's erotic behavior was modified only slightly after the letter. Further, reports began to circulate that such behavior carried over into his activities as a military chaplain, where he served in the national guard. He had reached a high rank and had done enough favors for commanding officers to avoid any official disfavor.

A fine academic ceremony marked this professor's retirement from the seminary faculty. He then became an occasional visiting professor at several seminaries.

Sexual philandering, as it was more tastefully termed in more male-dominant days, is still not unusual in academic settings, including seminaries. Some of the most illustrious names in theology have been tarnished by well-known sexual predation or extramarital affairs. Such eroticized behavior is also not unknown in denominational offices and chanceries. It is less likely now, however, due to heightened awareness and caution, as well as legal vulnerabilities. Recent scandals involving seminary presidents, at both conservative and progressive seminaries have caused great consternation. For there is a general awareness that sexual misconduct continues. Boards of trustees, however, may now present a president with evidence of sexual misconduct and require a letter of resignation.

My research, consultations, and court testimonies, along with media exposés have convinced me of the enormous moral devastation and staggering costs that result from high-level sexual predation, unless such consequences are controlled by hierarchical containment or intimidation. If we are to regain and retain professional and spiritual integrity, we must all accept responsibility for cleaning up our sordid moral scandals. Admissions of sexual conspiracies and public apologies are only a beginning for this mission.

Predation and exploitations by pastors of local congregations are still a public scandal, and somewhat less likely to be discovered or prosecuted than high-level sexual conspiracies. Much of the present research still suggests that a significant number of sexual predators continue to wreak their havoc, even when they are suspected of misconduct (for complete stories and review of this phenomenon, see Fortune 1999 and Rediger 1990). Codes of conduct, heightened awareness, and threat of negative consequences, which now deter some, are inadequate to deter hardcore predators. It is important to understand the ingrained nature of sexual predation and its perpetrators if we are determined to detect, discipline, and prevent further abuses. Correlative to our deeper understanding is care and support for victims. For predators know how to intimate, deny, and cover their boundary violations. Therefore the protected testimony and stories of victim-survivors is crucial to prosecution, to heightened awareness for congregations, pastors, and denominational offices, and to a fresh theology of healthy sexuality (more later). Most important is restoring the health and religious faith of victims so they may become healthy survivors.

The differentiation of sexual predators from pedophiles, molesters, and incest perpetrators is important, for detection and therapy of predators are typically less stringent (regimented and long-term) and prognosis more positive. The frequent presence of mental impairment, childhood abuse, and brooding focus on children are characteristic in pedophilia, molestations, and long-term incest (Axis I symptoms in DSM-IV). Again with a caution against seeking precise symptoms and behavior, sexual predators are more likely to exhibit personality disorders and inappropriate, compulsive behavior (Axis II symptoms in DSM-IV).

In more familiar terminology, we may list cognitive and behavioral characteristics that mark predators, such as the following (these are selected from a list devised to identify sexual abusers by Marie Fortune in her workshop manual [1997]). Her list of cognitive traits includes controlling, low insight, compulsive, charismatic, confuses sex with affection, poor judgment, and lack of empathy. To this list I would add cleverness, defined as an ability to contrive erotic relationships. Fortune also lists behavioral traits such as seeking and attracting vulnerable persons, being manipulative and secretive, along with an attitude that minimizes consequences. To this I would add that their whole life tends to be eroticized.

Sexual predators, as I am defining them, are difficult to capture, prosecute, and treat, not because they are difficult to see, but because they operate cleverly. They seek and relate to sexually needy persons who are likely to accept sexual assertiveness and even blame themselves for the abuse. Such victims are less likely to bring allegations of misconduct.

Sexual predators enjoy romantic playfulness and deny intentions of harm, thus seducing and confusing their prey. Sexual predators are often clever about covering or camouflaging their conquests, including convincing victims to be secretive, and that this is healthy or spiritual therapy. When confronted, they often have ingenious and distracting rationalizations.

The darkest dimension of sexual predation is rape and extended sexual abuse. Although rape, as it is currently defined, can seem to be consensual, or at least not resisted, it is still rape. In earlier times rape was defined as violent, sexual, and coercive. The sexual revolution has opened the opportunity for sexual intercourse to become a normal participatory sport, meaning anyone can do it, anywhere, as long as it is consensual. But this consensual aspect is problematic, for consent can be induced, mistaken, or transitory.

Legal and moral definitions of rape are still evolving. Defining rape now seems to be a right belonging to victim-survivors. Further, marital rape is newly defined as a crime comparable to other rapes in some states, while it is not a crime at all in two states (cited in Cooper-White 1995, 81).

Rape in or out of marriage is an especially difficult issue for African American women, for they often find that the men they relate to may presume the historic privilege of master to women slaves. In an interview with the Reverend Sharon Ellis, D.Min., former Chicago Police Chaplain and now an advocate for women in domestic violence at Trinity United Church of Christ, she observes that there are some black pastors who regard women in the congregation as sexually available to them. And after many years of this servitude, black women parishioners often try to make the best of this disrespect by competing for their pastor's favors. In her carefully researched book, *Sex, Lies, and Rabbis: Breaking a Sacred Trust* (2002), Charlotte Rolnick Schwab indicates that this entitlement attitude is not foreign to some rabbis. We should note here that these observations, though accurate, are not true for most pastors and rabbis. However, they add urgency to defining and enforcing professional boundaries.

According to the 1998 U.S. Department of Justice's "National Violence against Women Survey," 18 percent of women surveyed reported they had experienced an attempted or completed rape at some time in their lives. For 22 percent of this group, this occurred before they were twelve years of age. These troubling statistics have another side, for the horror such abuse imposes on women can only be done by socially and psychologically impaired men, or those who themselves are victims of social programming built on male dominance. In order to help lessen and end rape, the church must avoid the trap of demonizing such men as monsters, which then allows us to ignore the everyday realities of intimate violence in the home, church, neighborhood, and workplace, where the offenders are typically "nice" men or "safe" clerics. For most rape is committed by persons known by the victims. This suggests that while criminal punishment is important, therapy and radically improved training of young males is required for long-range improvement (summarized from Livingston 2002).

Men, of course, are raped, too, usually when they are young, although the incidence is less. The effects, however, are similar (more later).

Two illustrative cases may aid in understanding the complexity and pain of these issues when church professionals are involved.

Friendly Rape

A pastor's wife made counseling appointments with me in order to sort out the behavior of her husband, not only with her, but with a close family friend. She reported that she and her husband had fallen into the "Not tonight, honey . . . I have a headache" syndrome. She said she realized this was not a healthy management of marital sex, but she had developed this excuse because she found their sex life boring and focused only on her husband's orgasms and pleasure. After months of her excuses, and his growing agitation, he finally coerced her into sexual intercourse, by using guilt trips and suggestions that he may find his sexual satisfactions elsewhere. She succumbed, and reported that she even found their renewed sexual experiences somewhat welcome again, especially because of his passionate aggressiveness.

Then one hot summer afternoon, as she and a dear friend were sitting in the living room in their swimsuits and sipping gin and tonic, her husband casually entered the room in the nude. He joined them with his gin and tonic and began friendly banter that became more sexually explicit. Soon he got up, went over to their friend seated on a couch, began to caress her, and then slowly moved her into a supine position, removed her swimsuit, and had sexual intercourse with her. Shortly thereafter, he moved over to where his spouse was seated and repeated the sexual encounter, as if this was all normal behavior.

After telling me of this experience in a counseling appointment, she told of phone conversations subsequent to the dual rape in her home. She said she and her friend tried to figure what had happened. But both agreed this was unwanted male dominance. For they both had been caught off guard, had been drinking, and did not know how to object to this pastor's aggression. I commented that this is why more advocates for women and experienced therapists are calling such experiences rape. I told her my working definition of rape, which is the coercive use of another individual for sexual gratification. With a look of sudden recognition, she agreed that what she had experienced was rape and would continue to be rape if her husband insisted on his version of marital intercourse.

At her insistence, this pastor joined her for a couple appointments. He freely admitted the sexual encounter and continuing marital conflict, even agreeing that what he did to their friend was against his denomination's code of conduct. Instead of contrition, however, he insisted there was another perspective to all this. He refused to participate in further counseling. And after a couple more counseling appointments, she indicated that she now felt clear and confident about what she must do.

Shortly thereafter I learned that he had been moved to a congregation in another town. She remained behind and began divorce proceedings. I gave her the name of a woman psychiatrist who then assisted her in dealing with a resultant depression. In a later note to me she told how her friend was also in therapy, and urged me to help the church and clergy understand the seriousness of rape, not only from abusive male predators, but also from the seemingly normal, competent male pastors who "just don't get it."

Executive Rape

In another case, I accepted a counseling commitment with a woman pastor who was divorced, with two young children, and in her mid-thirties. She reported on a sexual relationship she was having with her district superintendent. In her view this relationship had developed into a deep, romantic commitment, even though this church executive was married. She now expected him to divorce his wife and marry her. But he was resisting. He tried to apologize to her and then end the relationship. She insisted that he had made a commitment to marriage, as she had. And now she was insisting he continue their sexual relationship and marry her, or she would tell his spouse, and report him to their bishop. I asked her if this sounded like rape to her. She denied this indignantly, declaring that it may be intimidation but not rape.

He agreed to meet with us, and he told his side of the story. He apologized profusely to her but declared that he could not leave his wife. The bishop already knew, he told her, for he had informed him of this relationship recently. The bishop indicated that if the district superintendent stayed with his wife, and if they both kept this issue secret, he would continue their appointments in their present charges.

When she heard this, she became both angry and contrite. I worked with them for several more appointments as they dealt with their mixed emotions, and then agreed to the bishop's mandate. For some months thereafter, I counseled separately with this woman pastor and with the district superintendent and his spouse. The outcomes seemed satisfactory to all parties.

Variations on these cases continue to be lived out every day. But we turn now to the second insidious classification included in this grouping of sexual predation and sexual addiction. Note again that these are grouped loosely together because of personality disorder, uncontrolled sexual compulsion, and habitual eroticizing of natural sexual desires and intimate relationships. The second type in this grouping can be described as sexual addiction.

Sexual addiction is a controversial classification, which is easily understood. In my judgment, therapists who claim that addiction is the primary dynamic of most sexual misconduct are helping organized religion understand why codes of conduct and simplistic therapies are inadequate for controlling much of clergy sexual misconduct. Other therapists and researchers, myself included, however, believe that the addiction model introduces serious misconceptions. I intend to make the case that sexual misconduct is more complicated and variable than the addiction model suggests.

Patrick Carnes, a dedicated proponent of the addiction model, defines sexual addiction as a pathological relationship with a mood-altering experience, much like alcoholism (see *Out of the Shadows: Understanding Sexual Addiction* [1994]). He goes on to show that this addiction is a substitution of habitual eroticism for healthy intimate relationships. His recommended treatment regimen is primarily the Alcoholics Anonymous Twelve-Step program.

Nils Friberg and Mark Laaser offer a modified addiction viewpoint that allows for other causes, such as environmental influences, "situational and transient difficulties," and the one-time offender. Yet in their book *Before the Fall: Preventing Pastoral Sexual Abuse* (1998), the addiction model is their primary reference point for understanding and managing clergy sexual misconduct.

Pamela Cooper-White, in *The Cry of Tamar* (1995), argues that the addiction model presents sexual misconduct as a physiological disease, which allows a clergyperson so afflicted to escape responsibility for his behavior. Further, this model does not address a male power addiction because it does not confront societal forces that proffer dominance of men over women. She concludes that a total paradigm shift is needed. For treating these problems as sexual immorality, emotional instability, or addiction does not address the male power dynamics of these often hidden abuses.

In my experience the addiction model offers valuable insights into the compulsive nature of some sexual misconduct and also provides the effective Twelve-Step program for stringent therapy and supervision. When the addiction model is posited as a primary perspective, however, it does tend to offer recourse to disease as an excuse from personal responsibility and discounts the effects of societal injustice. Although it provides a reminder of the potency of human appetites, it generates a curious implication, namely, that since we are all addicted to something that seems to meet our powerful appetites, such as food, TV, love, and money, we should therefore all be in Twelve-Step programs. Some have argued that the exclusiveness of the addiction model indicts all frequent drinkers.

The following case from my files may illustrate the use of available resources besides the Twelve-Step program.

The Case of the
Sexually Obsessed Pastor

A pastor approaching midlife began to phone our office incessantly asking for advice for how to get his wife to respond more compliantly to his sexual needs. I encouraged him to make an appointment, and he did. When he arrived for his first appointment he was so intent on telling his story, with vivid details, that we had difficulty completing the intake process.

Without hesitation or embarrassment he told me of their almost daily conflict. He would come home late afternoon and play or work with their three children for a while, then begin his hints that he would like to go to the bedroom for sex. She would discourage this while continuing to prepare dinner, or whatever else was on her agenda. After dinner and evening meetings or work with the children, he would begin to talk sex to her until bedtime. This became the sole agenda for our counseling appointments. Occasionally he would interrupt his recitation to assure me that he restrained his sex talk when the children were close by.

After several appointments in which he did nearly all the talking, and repeated his plea for help in making his spouse more compliant, he became bored, and shifted to telling me about his small-town parish, and a couple of attractive women he was friendly with in town. When I asked whether any of these friendships were sexual, he affirmed without hesitation that they were, and that even though he did not often arrange for sex with these women, they always seemed very compliant sexually.

When I suggested that we invite his spouse to join us in appointments, he agreed eagerly. In her first visit, she was shy and soft-spoken. I asked her why she thought this man made appointments to see me. She quickly answered that he told her it was about her and sex. I asked for her version of their relationship, and she began to cry softly, as she did often in subsequent appointments. Then she told me she tried to make him happy sexually and was willing to have sex several times a week. But she couldn't handle every night, and sometimes during the day. When he interrupted her to say he only wanted sex once each night, she suddenly screamed at him, "Get off my back!"

At my suggestion, and with her agreement, I met with her for a couple of appointments alone. Her story of childhood in a hardworking, joyless family, and now her husband's incessant sexual demands, as well as her day job, family care, and required attendance at church functions left her exhausted much of the time. She expressed appreciation for my listening to her story, and said it felt like such a relief to be able to tell her story to someone who cared. Then she said, "Please help us."

They both agreed to my suggestion to join a therapy-support group that I facilitated with another pastoral counselor. The group was composed of several professional couples, who received them cordially. This pastor immediately dominated the group for a couple of sessions with his complaints about his wife. Toward the end of a third group meeting with them, one of the wives, a sophisticated, recovering alcoholic, told him to stop and listen to her. Then she said slowly and emphatically, "You are a sex addict!" The pastor was quiet for the rest of the session.

The next week he sat quietly for a while, as others told their stories. Then he said, "Last week I heard the voice of God . . . finally." He thanked the woman who had confronted him and indicated that he needed the group's help in learning how to manage his sexual addiction. They unanimously agreed to support him, if he would be willing to listen and learn while the group also processed their individual needs. He agreed. His wife, after a long time of uncontrolled weeping, said that for the first time in years she was feeling hopeful.

In a combination of weekly therapy-support group meetings and alternating appointments as a couple and individually, they made steady progress, until we could invite the children to join us, as we developed a family-therapy model together. After nearly two years in this combination, they indicated enough confidence to terminate appointments. A few months later, the group gave them a fond farewell and invited them to "sit in" occasionally. The pastor became part of a clergy group that met regularly. His spouse helped develop a women's book club in the community. The children showed no signs of impairment from their parents' sexual conflict.

He and his spouse ended his casual relationships with the two divorced women in the community as honorably as they could by going to them and apologizing sincerely. Both women were willing to settle the issue this way, for they each had developed other relationships that were moving toward marriage.

All cases of clergy sexual addiction do not end comfortably. The case of the researcher married to a battering rabbi (Schwab 2002) is a horrifying story of combined predation, sexual addiction, and battering. Schwab tells her own story of a rabbi who was able to maintain himself as competent and caring to his congregation and community while leading a double life, unknown to spouse, colleagues, and congregation. When Schwab became aware and strong enough to confront him, he resorted to emotional and physical battering that continued for several years, in spite of her pleas and suffering. It all ended in lawsuits, formal charges, and destructive recriminations. Not until she undertook strong confrontational actions and divorced him was the truth exposed and her suffering ended. She has since devoted her career to such confrontations and advocacy for abused spouses of rabbis. Besides living this torture, she has compiled lengthy lists of media reports, research documents, books and articles, and personal stories of battered spouses of rabbis.

My files confirm such tortuous experiences among pastors in Protestantism. I still recall the shock as I visited in the home of a well-known pastor of a tall-steeple church, with whom I had become friendly. While sipping coffee in this couple's living room, I overheard, through closed bedroom doors, him shouting at her and the crashing of thrown objects. He came out to continue our visit as if nothing was wrong. But I began to notice thereafter (what I had apparently overlooked before) her occasional limps, her use of cosmetics to hide bruises, and the haunting look in her eyes. She later died of unexplained circumstances.

In this part of the book I concentrate on major types of distorted sexuality. But I must note a subcategory of this "insidious sexual misconduct" grouping, namely, the "stalker." This is not a clinical term nor is it a distinct category of misconduct, for it occurs as part of major syndromes such as predator, addict, and, especially, batterer. There is not much research literature on it, for it is typically part of a larger syndrome. Yet it is a distinctive behavior, described by its name. Its notoriety derives from media coverage of celebrities being stalked, and from a fascination with its shadowy mysteries.

Approximately one million women are stalked annually, according to the "National Violence against Women Survey" (Department of Justice 1998). Statistics on men being stalked are not clear. Stalking is a tactic rather than a singular behavior. Stalkers trail and signal their prey in order to achieve a goal.

In my experience, there are three types of stalkers: those who stalk to gain information and build a case against someone (for example, surveillance by detectives or agents); those who stalk in order to stay in touch with someone because of love or fascination; and those who are desperate because of being forced out of an intimate relationship. The latter type is the dangerous one who might commit serious harm or murder. Such a person feels desperately alone and abandoned and thus is driven by survival instincts (an insight borrowed from Livingston 2002). The other two types may engage in mischief or try to manipulate the prey but are more annoying than dangerous.

My experience includes being stalked by a disgruntled client. I had aided his spouse in freeing herself from his domination. He followed me on numerous occasions, by car, by telephone calls demonstrating he knew where I was, and by messages left with persons who would relay them without suspecting his motivations. I had an advantage in having done therapy with him, and therefore was reassured by understanding his key motivations and thought patterns. Yet his stalking was unnerving at times and frustrating in that I could not seek assistance without breaking confidentiality. He was finally assigned to a distant parish, and I never heard from him again.

Although the number of clergy who are predators, addicts, and batterers may be relatively small, the damage they cause is enormous. Organized religion has only one honorable course.

Summary

This chapter is a painful exploration of both the camouflaged front side of clergy sexual predation—rape, addiction, and domestic battering—and the dark side that deviates shockingly from acceptable clergy behavior. The difficulties in defining both the terminology and categorizing of such complex abuses are reviewed. Clinical and spiritual dynamics are discussed, and brief cases are presented for illustration. Throughout these pained thoughts and information is an urgent prayer that their messages will be heard.

6. DISSONANT SEXUAL EXPRESSIONS

I DESIGNATE the next group of sexual categories as "dissonant" sexual expressions. This suggests that, while each is variable and clinically and socially distinct, they have in common a highly significant characteristic, namely, they are in some measure out of harmony with traditional, contemporary, and/or religious mores.

Dissonant here means unusual, variant, divergent, only in the sense of being different from what is considered acceptable in a traditional American setting. Behaviors included in this grouping draw mixed reactions and are judged differently by different segments of society. Their acceptability depends upon a nebulous sense of indifference, naïveté, bias, prejudice, participation, or moral judgment. Each has negative and positive potentials, and each is undergoing evaluation as American mores and theology are in transition.

The focus will be on the dark side of each of these sexual categories, for this is a central purpose of this book. But the potential for good, though sometimes small, will be mentioned. For we are learning that there is good and bad in everyone, and good and bad in nearly any experience.

Do not miss the warnings and dangers in each of these dissonances. If you find yourself fitting into the dark side of any of
these dissonances, seek professional assistance before the dark
side becomes your disaster. And if you are a victim of anyone who
practices one or more of these dissonances, seek professional
guidance for protecting yourself and those dear to you and in finding therapeutic aid for the person enmeshed in the dark side.

Cybersex

The term *cybersex* is new, originating in the age of computers.
Essentially, it designates the erotica available on the internet, the
sexual interaction with the material, and persons ready to share
this experience. More generally, cybersex designates the physical,
mental, and spiritual experience of sex without love.

Pornography is the pejorative term usually used to designate
graphic sexuality. It is part of a larger category we know as erotica.
This more inclusive term includes all the art forms that have been
used to depict, write, speak, or sing about sexuality. Erotica is as historic as the human development of drawing and writing and making
music. The Bible includes erotica as well as proscriptions and moral-
izations on sexuality. From the Garden of Eden to stories of rape and
infidelity, the rhapsodies of the Song of Solomon, the ministries of
Jesus to prostitutes, the sexual anxieties of the Apostle Paul, the per-
sonification of "abomination" in the "last days" as the "Great
Whore," our holy book tells of the human joys and abuses of sexuality. In secular art we have nude statues, the poetry of Ovid, paint-
ings of Andrew Wyeth, novels of John Updike, and some kinds of
jazz and rap music—to mention only a few of the most acceptable
artists. We live with the mix of healthy and unhealthy sexuality daily.

One of the realities of erotica is that it connects sexuality and
spirituality—sometimes in debauched and oppressive ways, sometimes in beautiful and celebrative ways. When we bring a puritan-

ical perspective to erotica we are in danger of distorting or eliminating what is good and beautiful as well as circumscribing what is debasing. Censorship, inquisition, secrecy, and hypocrisy follow. When we bring a libertarian perspective to erotica we are in danger of desecrating what is beautiful, romantic, and uplifting. Indulgence, disrespect, rationalizing, and brutalization follow.

Fear and dualism (separating body and spirit) have generated excessive anxiety and legalism regarding sexuality in Western civilization for centuries. In the latter half of the last century the sexual revolution erupted with both excesses and fresh appreciation of the physical, mental, and spiritual realities of sexuality in all of creation. A major spiritual responsibility for this generation is to use a brand new medium to find a healthy mix of freedom and responsibility as we enjoy God's gift of sexuality.

The limited positive potential of cybersex is that in a healthier form it could be a form of entertainment, related to God's gift of sexuality. In its responsible use it has positive possibilities, such as sex education, sex therapy, marital enhancement, and helping to provide a sexual dynamic for our understanding of spirituality.

Cybersex is also pornography, at least in its most common forms today. Already its potential for exploitation, addiction, and oppression is developing into an epidemic of dissipation. We will need courage and spiritual discernment to intervene to protect victims and to develop the positive uses we have found for computerized ministries in other fields, such as education, family entertainment, evangelization, and celebrations of beauty. Evil is well ahead of us at present in the quest to shape cybersex for the future.

Cybersex is so new that research has not caught up with all its effects. So far, however, it is clear that some people stumble across it accidentally, and are shocked or intrigued or dismayed. For some, such sights trigger deep, painful, confused feelings. Others get their spouse and watch it together. Still others look, turn away, then occasionally look again for a brief kick. For a healthy few, there is respectful excitement regarding positive uses of cybersex for the benefit of humankind. Yet for many, the first look is the beginning of an enslavement. We have not prepared well for this sudden revisitation of the Garden of Eden.

A major theme of this book is the need to understand both the dark side and the enlightened side of sexuality, as it blends with spirituality. In this chapter I continue to examine the data, behaviors, and distortions of human sexuality, as presently practiced in North America. Even in its early stages of development, cybersex has generated significant insights and data that help us understand its potential for sin and evil. (There is much less information about its positive uses, which I will discuss later.)

Probably the most significant aspect in the emergence of cybersex is "the triple A engine" that drives it: availability, affordability, and anonymity (cited from Schneider and Weiss 2001). To this I would add excitement, a general euphoria akin to what Schneider and Weiss call "the trance." This is the quick gratification cybersex can provide, on demand. I would also add the attraction of hassle-free, "virtual love," in which sexual disappointments with a marriage partner can be bypassed. Then there is the popularization of cybersex, in which it seems "everyone is doing it," and this somehow helps rationalize the negative consequences. These six characteristics of cybersex nearly tell the whole story of its massive appeal.

Millions of people now use the Internet daily, and the numbers are growing. Access is easy and quick for adults—and for children, who seem to have been born with a computer for a brain. The cost in dollars is modest—mostly the one-time cost of a computer. There are no expensive 900 phone number calls to make, no drives to porno stores or prostitutes to pay. But it is the anonymity and secrecy that really makes cybersex attractive. For it is available anywhere there is Internet access, twenty-four hours a day, with no need for anyone to help or know (unless the hard drive is searched). In secret and alone, the user can do nearly anything that suits his or her fancy (some polls of Internet users show that 45 percent of those who logged on for cybersex are women and 38 percent men).

As I do seminars and conferences for clergy and denominational officials around the U.S., I hear more and more stories about clergy indulgence in cybersex. This concerns me, not only because cybersex in its present form is debasing and dangerous but also because clergy have many ways to indulge and imagine they are keeping this secret from everyone but themselves and the One who called us to be faithful and disciplined pastors.

The stories and pained confessions I hear have already fallen into a pattern. First, the pastor begins to consider the possibility of watching porn on the Internet. Then he or she thinks about how and where this indulgence can be kept secretive. By this time, rationalizations and anticipations are solidifying a decision to indulge. From then on, it's a matter of how often and how long. As noted earlier, most pastors who try cybersex do so once or intermittently, for they have enough common sense or spiritual discipline in their lives to avoid slipping into obsessive habits.

Consider what happens if pastoral indulgence begins to be reported regularly in the media. We already have an image problem because of many reports and rumors of clergy misconduct, along with frequent cover-ups. Now the image will not only be of our pastor molesting our children, or seducing our parishioners, or battering our pastor's wife, it could also become a mental image of our pastor sitting in our church office, watching pornography on our computer while masturbating.

Consider what happens to a clergy marriage when the spouse feels the lessening of romance and sexual satisfactions and begins to doubt herself or himself, or suspects the aging process or an extramarital affair, until catching the pastor-spouse indulging in cybersex.

Consider what happens when it dawns on the indulging pastor that an enslaving addiction has taken over his life that now distorts pastoral ministry. The guilt trips and anxiety over possibly being discovered waken him in a cold sweat some nights when he is too exhausted from indulging to sleep peacefully. Such a pastor now has another god to answer to. One offers forgiveness and healing. The other offers a life of dependence on cybersex for sexual gratification—until a disaster or a wake-up call.

Consider what happens when an indulging pastor begins to consider acting out his cybersex fantasies of meeting an Internet sex partner in person, or focusing a now out-of-control sexual obsession on a child or adult in the congregation.

The addiction model fits cybersex well, for cybersex appeases a deep human need, even if only temporarily. It is readily available. And continued indulgence soon builds a dependence that cannot be broken, no matter the warnings or consequences. Most pastors have had to deal with addictions of various sorts frequently enough to know the warning signs. But somehow, with enough stress, enough marital dissatisfaction, enough self-doubt, and inadequate spiritual disciplines, it is happening to us. As experts on addiction point out, addiction is relational. Cybersex can become a substitute for healthy relationships.

After many years of studying spiritual leadership roles and providing pastoral counseling and training to the human beings who are trying to be effective pastors, nothing concerns me more for the future of faithful pastoring than the availability of cybersex. Seminaries, denominational offices, clergy groups, and congregations need to recognize and exorcise this evil (remember the cautionary tale about the camel who puts its head into your tent).

The Paraphilias

Paraphilia is a clinical term meaning a condition in which a persistent fantasy involving an unusual object or human relationship is needed for sexual arousal. Most researchers will not estimate how many persons practice paraphilias, but it is apparent that more men than women practice these behaviors. John Money (1981) lists twenty-eight paraphilias, although more recently he has concentrated on categorizing these according to the objects or behavior that fuel the arousal fantasies. Alfred Kinsey, Money, and other researchers indicate the paraphilias are probably more common than expected, and typically male. There is no strong evidence regarding causes.

The DSM-IV establishes eight specific paraphilias and one general category (diagnoses summarized from James Morrison 2001):

1. Exhibitionism, the compulsion to expose genitals to unsuspecting strangers for arousal. Common; usually male; targets children or women; begins early in life but may last to midlife; occurrences when stressed; repetitive pattern often includes masturbation; alcohol not common; many married with normal sex lives; careful; seldom violent.

2. Fetishism, the attachment of magical fantasies to symbolic sex objects. Onset in adolescence; usually male; needs fetish for arousal; typically fixated on female underwear; handle or smell fetish while masturbating; often alone; chronic; fetish may replace healthy sexual relationship.

3. Frotteurism, physical erotic contact for sexual arousal. Occurs in crowds; usually male; begins in adolescence but continues into early adulthood; fantasizes relationship and masturbates; seldom violent.

4. Sexual masochism, the deriving of sexual pleasure from receiving varying degrees of pain. Begins in childhood; chronic; often requires increasing degrees of pain as in addiction; uses preplanned bondage, beating, cutting, humiliation; about 5 percent women; a few use the dangerous practice of hypoxyphilia (produce near asphyxiation by a noose around the neck or a plastic bag over the head or "poppers" [amyl nitrite]); often have a sadistic partner.

5. Sexual sadism, deriving sexual pleasure from inflicting varying degrees of pain. Similar to sexual masochism, except for role reversal; needs a willing partner, sometimes a prostitute, but may coerce or rape; can become brutal.

6. **Transvestic fetishism,** in which a heterosexual male recurrently seeks and experiences sexual pleasure by fantasizing sex acts while cross-dressing. Begins in early adolescence; uses varying numbers of female garments, often worn underneath their male clothing; frustrated when this behavior is opposed; may use elaborate rituals, developing into full public dressing as females; may masturbate or have intercourse when cross-dressed; is secretive; typically not effeminate; a few may dress completely as women and become transsexual; often participate in the significant transvestite subculture; seldom uses violence.

7. **Voyeurism,** being sexually aroused by watching people engaged in private behavior who do not know they are being watched. Begins in adolescence; masturbate while observing; becomes chronic; almost all are male; may fantasize sexual relationship with the prey, but seldom pursues it; secretive; usually has a relatively normal sex life besides the paraphilia.

8. **Pedophilia** is included in many lists of paraphilia, including DSM-IV. I understand that pedophilia/ephebophilia has similarities with paraphilias, but in my experience it differs significantly in that it targets children for sexual abuse, it often includes mental impairment, it is usually chronic, it is insidious and abusive even when threatened with discovery, and its recidivism rate is especially high.

9. **Paraphilia not otherwise specified,** a general classification for paraphilia that do not meet criteria for any of the specific categories. This includes telephone scatologia (making obscene phone calls), necrophilia (attraction to corpses), zoophilia (attraction to animals), and others.

A Pastor's Cross-Dressing Secret

I offer a case study of this paraphilia because it is relatively common, is often misunderstood, and likely occurs more frequently among clergy than most other paraphilias.

A pastor arrived for an appointment accompanied by his wife. The man was physically large, and his bearing was commanding, even intimidating. But he was friendly and immediately responsive.

He stated his case matter-of-factly. For years he had practiced cross-dressing. He particularly liked to dress in women's silky undergarments and pantyhose, and he nearly always did this before sex with his wife. Only when he did this was he able to enjoy orgasm.

His discomfort was with his obsessiveness about cross-dressing, not with his sexual identity, he informed me. Shame was not a significant factor. He was worried that his practices might be discovered by outsiders, and he was concerned because his sexual behavior did not fit his professional or personal ethics.

When he finished telling his story, I asked his wife why she had come. She said that she also would like these practices to cease. He had done this cross-dressing without her knowledge for years, and he had told her about it only a year ago. She was shocked, hurt, and disgusted at first, she reported, but had reluctantly come to accept it. She had gotten past blaming herself and questioning their love for each other. In fact, she had come to accept his cross-dressing in her presence before intercourse, and even helped him dress in her undergarments on occasion.

It became apparent that they had a good, intimate relationship. The future of their marriage did not depend on his ending the transvestism, although both wanted this. I suggested taking a sexual history from both of them, and they agreed to do this in each other's presence.

Their sexual histories contained no dramatic experiences. His relationship to his parents, however, contained some of the classic sexual material associated with transvestism and some other sexual disorders—a distant relationship with his father, a very close relationship with his mother, and emotional distance between his parents. His mother was seductive. When they were in the house alone, she would sometimes bathe with the bathroom door open. Occasionally she would give him an armload of her undergarments and ask him to launder them. They never had any physical, sexual contact with each other, but there was an erotic attachment neither of them talked about.

Both pastor and spouse had been in counseling on other occasions. They were alert to the issues, so we discussed strategies. It was apparent that both wanted change, but there appeared to be no urgent motivation for change. Their relationship was good, both were satisfied in their careers, and there appeared to be little danger of discovery or scandal. When I commented on this, he calmly indicated that he had a strong will and was accustomed to disciplining himself rigorously. She shed some tears at this time and said she really hoped they could achieve a normal marriage.

We decided on a fourfold strategy. First, he would practice imagining his cross-dressing ritual without actually doing it, and then see if their lovemaking could be satisfying. Along with this, they agreed to increase their foreplay. This was to include enjoying sensual things together (music, food, wine, fragrances, and so forth) prior to intercourse. They agreed to shower together and do full body massages several times a week, whether or not this led to intercourse. They did this for several months and found that he was unable to sustain an erection most of the time. Still, they felt some progress was being achieved.

Second, we decided that he needed to work again on his relationship to his parents. His mother had died, and his father was mentally disabled in a nursing home, so he wrote daily letters to each parent. For several weeks this pastor reviewed childhood memories, vented deep boyhood fear and anger, and then told his parents what he wanted to happen between them. The letters released some inner tensions, and there was some lessening of the pastor's cross-dressing.

Third, although we had discussed the theological, ethical, and spiritual dimensions of this situation during our appointments, we had not emphasized them. At this point, however, I felt that his spirituality could become a valuable and fundamental resource in resolving the conflict. We took some time to explore meditative-devotional exercises, and drew up a schedule for establishing them in daily practice. The relaxation, reassurance, and dependability of these exercises further improved the situation.

Finally, we decided that one of the reinforcing elements of the old pattern was the familiarity of ritual. The couple exchanged bedrooms with one of their children. They redecorated and arranged the room in ways that were relaxing and sensuous. They also experimented with some different ways of foreplay and intercourse. It took a number of months to break some of the old patterns and establish a new style of physical intimacy, but they reported success in achieving a happier relationship.

Although the estimate of one million transvestites in America seems relatively small, the practice is well established. Some clergy are transvestites. My experience indicates that the transvestite pastor will be as competent, friendly, caring, and dedicated to ministry as the nontransvestite.

As this case study indicates, the pastoral counseling method of choice is to reduce anxiety, offer ways to change if they are desired, and give the spouse every support technique appropriate to her needs. The marriage may have to exist with some distortions, as many marriages do. But reassurance, support, and guidance can aid the person who is a transvestite and his marriage partner to have a satisfying life and ministry.

Sexual Dysfunctions

We need to be concerned about sexual dysfunctions among clergy, because clergy are human beings first and clergy second. This means they are likely to experience the same sexual dysfunctions as nonordained persons do. We also need to be concerned because sexual dysfunctions affect us in primal-preconscious levels as well in conscious-behavior levels. This means they are capable of sabotaging sexual health and distorting ministry long-term as well as in the present. Further, since we seldom talk about sexual issues (except to argue about homosexuality, abortion, and abstinence) in the synagogue or church, we may not know or understand our sexual dysfunctions. At present we do not even know whether to call sexual dysfunctions sin or immorality or evil, much less do we have a realistic theology of healthy sexuality (more on this later). I hope this brief review of sexual dysfunctions helps precipitate open discussion and a fresh look at the theological as well as clinical implications.

In the DSM-IV the listed sexual dysfunctions are essentially medical-clinical diagnostic classifications. A full discussion is beyond the purview of this book. They are listed here for quick information and as a reminder of conditions that medical and mental health professionals see as sexual dysfunctions.

1. Hypoactive sexual desire disorder, recurrent, deficient (or absent) sexual fantasies and desire for sexual activity. An implication exists that an absence or deficiency of sexual fantasy and desire is abnormal. This speaks directly to our typical clergy guilt trips and puritanical presumptions. It also implies that we are missing something important if we do not own and celebrate sexual passions in our theology and ministries. Yet this is a disorder for some.

2. Sexual aversion disorder, persistent, extreme aversion to all sexual contact with a sexual partner. Such a condition may be valuable to those who have taken a vow of celibacy, but it is regarded professionally as detrimental to healthy sexuality. The implications are that though it is normal to avoid or dislike sex occasionally, something unhealthy is involved if persistent aversion develops.

3. Female sexual arousal disorder, persistent or recurrent inability to attain or maintain an adequate lubrication-dilation response of sexual excitement. Such inadequacies clearly affect sexual intimacy. Moreover, these are indicators of many possible prejudices, injustices, and distorted beliefs about female sexuality and the emotions that promote it. The reality that media and sex education give much more attention to male sexual disorders than to those that trouble women is a reminder of social and religious biases.

4. Male erectile disorder, persistent or recurrent inability to attain or maintain a penile erection up to completion of the sexual activity. The jokes and pharmacological attention devoted to this dysfunction imply more than we may have noticed about the presumptions of traditional gender perspectives in society and organized religion. Female sexual disorders, by comparison, are not presumed to be significant.

5. Female orgasmic disorder, persistent or recurrent delay in or absence of orgasm, following a normal sexual excitement phase. Before Johnny Carson discovered "the G spot," and infused it into America's humor on "The Tonight Show," there was little concern for female orgasm. By implication we can remind ourselves that humor is one way to learn about sexuality. It is more relevant to apply clinical information and caring spiritual discernment to factors that interfere with the sexual pleasure of women.

6. Male orgasmic disorder, persistent or recurrent delay in or absence of orgasm, following a normal sexual excitement phase. The presence of this diagnosis is a reminder not only that there can be orgasmic disorder for both women and men, but also that this is a serious and frustrating reality for a significant number of persons. By implication it also validates and celebrates the pleasure of orgasmic sexual experience. Another implication, however, is a discounting of sexual contact, stimulation, and shared intimacy in which orgasm is not necessarily an expectation.

7. Premature ejaculation, persistent or recurrent ejaculation with minimal sexual stimulation, or before it is desired. Because this experience is common and not desirable, it is a reminder that human beings do not engage in sexual activities with a guarantee of perfection. These sexual dysfunctions are as real as idealized sexual activities. They need not be embarrassing or shameful, but should be noted and treated if persistent.

8. Dyspareunia, persistent or recurrent pain associated with sexual intercourse in either male or female. Pain has often had different meanings, as well as being a different experience for males and females in human history. How often has female pain, needs, and functions been repressed or ignored in human history, and among religious professionals? This is worth conscious attention.

9. Vaginismus, persistent or recurrent involuntary spasm in the musculature of the outer area of the vagina that interferes with sexual intercourse. This dysfunction, as well as the others, may be caused by medical, psychological, or unknown inducements, of long-standing or temporary duration. This female malady is a reminder that both the female and the male partner in sexual intimacy are likely to experience discomfort when this dysfunction occurs—she physical pain and mental distress, he mental frustration and the stress of self-control while comforting her.

10. Substance-induced sexual dysfunction, marked distress or interpersonal difficulty in achieving sexual satisfaction due to intoxication. This experience is a reminder that the consequences of one "pleasure" can sabotage another. It makes a memorable case for moderation, and willingness to make the best of each other's over-indulgences. But it also can be a wake-up call for attention to addictive behaviors.

Sexual Harassment

Few issues point as clearly to the sexist core of organized religion as does sexual harassment. It is an attitude, a presumption; it is prejudice writ large; it is abusive; it is a violation of healthy religion and of God's purposes. Given our global tradition of sexism, such a statement may seem like an overreaction; it is intentionally broad. For a massive overreaction is often needed to transform any prejudiced social presumption. I make these statements not because I am liberated and unprejudiced (I wish I were, but I am only working on it), but because I recall so often sitting in pastoral counseling appointments with clergy who are women and wondering what their lives and ministry would have been like if they had had the full privileges accorded most men. And I do not yet know how to write about this issue, for I am a man.

Sexual harassment, a relatively new concept, is one person's (society's, religion's) imposition on another of any unacceptable eroticized communication or activity. Yet it is far more than offensive behavior. It is a mind-set, an attitude, a presumption of what is "normal." Harassment can be a matter of a risqué joke or pinup, an unacceptable glance, a personal innuendo, overly solicitous behavior, an unwelcome touch, hug, or kiss, attempted seduction, stalking, or rape. Just as powerfully, harassment can be hypocrisy, denial, ignoring gender issues, feigning support for women's issues (à la Trent Lott's demurrer on racism), pretending predatory behavior and sexist humor is all in jest, or a simple mistake (à la Bill Clinton's defense of sexist behavior), and officiating in the church or synagogue as if feminism is just another troubling issue to be resolved by male authority. It's not about a stated intention (men are good at denial) but about what happens. However subtle or blatant, whatever the degrees of seriousness one might attach to various words or actions, what makes it sexual harassment is that it is unacceptable to the person on the receiving end. And, it is a violation of our stewardship of a sexual (relational) creation.

Sexual harassment has much in common with rape, the root meaning of which is to steal, to seize. When we are tempted to think it is an overstatement to say sexual harassment is like rape, we can remind ourselves what we are learning about rape, namely, that it is more than physical abuse. Rape is violation of body-mind-spirit. Sexual harassment is not a diminutive of rape, it is a stealing or seizing of a mind and spirit that has serious consequences for the body. "A mind is a terrible thing to waste," said the TV ad promoting support for African American advanced education. This would be a worthy mantra in promoting the liberation of female pastors and the reeducation of male pastors.

We must note, of course, that women can harass men, gay men can harass gay men, lesbians can harass lesbians, and all can harass and kill in the home, in the workplace, and in society as an expression of repressed sexual motivations. And we must note that sexuality can be expressed in playful and supportive ways. The necessary ingredient for avoiding sexual harassment, even when there is playful intent, is the conscious recognition of each participant's comfort level.

In the church we consider ourselves moral and caring. It is often difficult for male clergy to believe that they might be involved in sexual harassment. But they have been involved for centuries, and today, even as the gender revolution is helping women to act freely in the management of their sexuality, harassment by males continues. In fact, the sexual revolution makes some men think that they can get away with more. Let us be very clear about a crucial truth: many women do insist that they have the right to be sexually active outside marriage, and that sex is something they have a right to enjoy, but that does not make them fair game for any man. The whole point of the gender and the sexual revolutions, in fact, is just the opposite.

When we are tempted to think sexual harassment may be nothing more than a rueful complaint from frustrated women, a guilt trip for men, or a passing social fad, we can regain reality by noting that the courts and legislatures of our land have not only legitimized and defined this issue but also are establishing penalties for offenders. The *Dictionary of Feminist Theologies* (Russell and Clarkson 1996) includes in its definition of sexual harassment the mandate of the U.S. Federal Equal Employment Opportunity Commission, 1990, which declares that sexual harassment is "the use of one's authority or power, either explicitly or implicitly, to coerce another into unwanted sexual relations or to punish another for his or her refusal; or the creation of an intimidating, hostile, or offensive working environment through verbal or physical conduct of a sexual nature."

Moreover, we have reliable data, besides the anecdotes and court cases, regarding the proportions of this offense in organized religion. Alongside of data from the secular workplace, we have statistics from church and synagogue. In her training manual, Marie Fortune (1997) lists several percentages of the harassment clergywomen have reported. In a 1996 United Church of Christ survey, 48 percent experienced sexual harassment by male clergy in the church workplace. A 1991 Unitarian Universalist survey indicated 21 percent of their women surveyed had experienced sexual harassment by clergy or lay leaders. A 1993 survey of female rabbis found that 29 percent had experienced sexual harassment by another rabbi. A 1990 survey of church workers by the United Methodist Church reported that 77 percent of their clergywomen experienced sexual harassment in the church.

In this time of interactive change, sexual issues have become more complex. Unrelated men and women work side by side in many occupations, and it has become increasingly acceptable for them to be close friends. The line between teamwork and friendship can become blurred, and friendship can turn into sexual involvement. But as the following case study shows, manipulation of the situation can be a most subtle and cruel kind of harassment

In our first appointment, a midlife woman told of her impending divorce from a clergy spouse after nearly thirty years of marriage and five children. She had finished her first year at seminary and was assigned to a reputable midlife pastor of a midsized congregation for mentoring. He was exceptionally cordial and helpful in the first weeks of their professional relationship.

At his invitation she rode with him to a regular denominational meeting. As they rode together he was solicitous of her comfort. After the meeting he took her to a fine restaurant for dinner. Then as they drove home, she mentioned being tired, and he invited her to lay her head on his shoulder.

There were subsequent trips and cordial office conversations. He invited her to preach and to lead meetings. She began to feel

indebted to him, and thought of him affectionately as a father figure. So entranced was she by this mentor relationship that she
barely resisted his hand on her thigh while driving to a meeting, or
his frequent hugs in the office. She awakened to her plight only
when they had sex.

Her divorce had become hostile, and her husband threatened to
tell the judge of what he believed was her sexual relationship with
her mentor. She began to recognize her victimization and called
my office in near panic.

After hearing her story, I asked her what she was telling herself
about these circumstances, and what support she felt she needed. It
took her several appointments to clarify her feelings and expectations. A female co-therapist helped her declare her anger, guilt, and
confusion. A lawyer we suggested helped end her husband's intimidation. At church the sexual harassment continued, although she
begged and pleaded with her mentor to stop.

One afternoon I received a conference phone call from my co-
therapist, our intern client, and her bishop. She had gathered her
courage and gone to the bishop with her story. He corroborated
her story, and said he would have a meeting with her mentor very
soon and straighten all this out. The woman was transferred to
another parish within driving distance. She continued in counseling with us until she believed she was ready to manage her future
without such assistance. Her mentor/seducer was reprimanded
privately by the bishop, but he remained in the same parish with
no public scandal.

Such cases have become so common that we all know what
questions to ask and what actions to take—or do we? As you read
this story, what questions came to your mind? What answers did
you give yourself? How do you deal with the power and control
issues, the naïveté and violated trust, the self-doubts, the male
hierarchy doing business as usual. We can do better than this!

I have dealt with both heterosexual and homosexual harassment
cases involving male clergy and secretaries, custodians, adult and

child parishioners, and women clergy. With the increase in numbers of women clergy, there are cases of harassment by females. There are even cases of mutual harassment and of mutual seduction. All of these are essentially unhealthy. Most sexual harassment cases involving the clergy, however, remain the harassment of women by clergymen. The incredible variety of cases reminds us of the vulnerability of all humans and of the opportunities for abuse that go with the clergy role, whoever fills it.

Clergy and their victims may not recognize sexual harassment; they may also deny it. The church has a responsibility in this matter. It is not demeaning to the church and the clergy to speak openly about sexual harassment in the church. It is demeaning, unjust, and damaging to everybody not to address and rectify the problem. One of the clearest tasks emerging from our growing awareness of sexual harassment is the clarification, dissemination, and enforcement of codes of professional ethics for clergy, and the treatment of the causes and elimination of settings conducive to such behavior.

It is unrealistic for the church to assume that victims and perpetrators know their rights, know what is unacceptable behavior, know that investigation and discipline will be enforced, and know that appropriate therapies are available, unless this is stated clearly and authoritatively. We can and should expect good judgment in clergy. But the inadequacies of training, policy, disciplines, and sexual-spiritual support are still apparent.

Summary

In this chapter the secret, seductive life in cybersex is examined. Although the Internet is relatively new, pornography is not. Human vulnerability to this dark side of sexual expression is now a moral epidemic among clergy as well as the general population.

The clergy role, working conditions, and loss of spiritual disciplines make fertile ground for seeds of this new/old evil.

A review of the clinically described paraphilias, with definitions, characteristics, and a case study, provides an overview of a segment of the population, including clergy, who live a secret life of stealth, fantasy and distorted sexual expression.

This discussion of dissonant sexual behavior closes with a strong warning and discussion of sexual harassment. Although this may seem like a relatively harmless, everyday practice in public and private life, a sensitive consideration shows it to be a galvanizing call for clearer policies and focused training, for much more support to victim-survivors, and for denominational crusades for health sexuality.

7.
VICTIM-SURVIVOR: CARE AND PREVENTION

ORGANIZED RELIGION must face its dark side. The reality of sin and evil has not been factored realistically into theology and practice for many years. This neglect has left us with only sporadic discernment concerning our dark side, and therefore a shallow experience of the joys attendant to God's original blessing and continuing grace. Our thinking and experience of sexuality, in ourselves and in creation, has left it to the legal system to call us to accountability for our secret sins. Further, it seems that we need the consequences of global pornography (cybersex) and "unsafe sex" to call us from shrill judgmentalism and hypocrisy to discernment of God's gift of sexuality. We all, including myself, share responsibility for our sins, and for our healing and salvation.

Victimization is the murky core of religion's dark side. Turning children, women, and men into victims is the opposite of religion's declared mission. To victimize those who seek salvation, to deny our sin and shelter abusers, to pretend to care for justice, is nearly unthinkable. Thanks be to God, we are beginning to take our dark side seriously. A long, penitent path to salvation lies ahead.

Exorcism is an archaic and repellent word, yet it can be instructive for our time. This term refers to an evil presence in a human being and a spiritual ritual for removing it (Catholics retain such a ritual, as do some charismatic faith communities). Chapter five in Mark's Gospel shows the biblical steps for exorcism. First, name the demon. Second, cast it out (Jesus did this, and believers do so in his name). Third, put something better (salvation and mission) in its place. When we face and deal with persons who allow evil to possess them, we must relearn the lessons of spiritual warfare.

Given our current inadequate theologies and unhealthy management of clerical sexuality and boundaries, we need clear guidelines for the out-of-control aspects of clergy sexual practices. This chapter will summarize the prophetic and caring aspects of our interventions and therapies. Then we may turn from our dark side toward the "light" side of sexuality and wholeness.

Three Cases

This book describes multiple cases of clergy sexual offenses. Three cases can help us shift to a focus on the victim-survivors of such offenses. One highlights the childhood experience, the second the adult possibilities, and the third describes possible congregational responses to being victimized.

A Boy's Story: The Hierarchy Failed

One of the stories presented in the *Boston Globe*'s book *Betrayal* (Carroll et al. 2002) concerns an altar boy and his priest. Alone together in the church basement late at night, the priest sexually abuses this boy. The pastor of the parish came through in the process of locking up. He saw what was occurring, asked that they turn out the lights when they were finished, and then "turned his back on the victim" and left. An attitude of benign neglect was evident regarding widespread sexual abuse of children by priests.

"After that betrayal, his grades plummeted, his ambitions evaporated." Then came years of floundering as an itinerant hippie and then attempts to live a celibate, ascetic life. For two decades his shame and confusion haunted him into a reclusive life. Somehow he completed his education, started a family, and devoted himself to working with abused children.

This young man finally developed the courage to inform a deputy of the archdiocese of the sexual abuse he had suffered. His accusation was brushed off as a relationship that was misinterpreted as sexual. The deputy told him his story was not credible, because if a priest is guilty of sexual misconduct, the priest admits it. The young man said he felt as if he had been abused again in this rejection.

After being ignored for so long, even as other complaints against the offending priest surfaced, this young man engaged a lawyer. He suffered alone for years because he thought he was alone. By the time he complained, he knew there were hundreds like him. The bleeding stopped, but the wound remains.

Who Is Safe? A Woman's Story

Another story comes from my files and memories. It is about a woman still in the process of redeeming her life.

When the door to my reception room opened, I was just emerging from another room. She fixed her eyes on me and held me in an intense stare. Then she relaxed, smiled graciously, and introduced herself. After amenities and filling out the intake form, we proceeded into the consultation room and I closed the door.

She seated herself on the front edge of our large upholstered chairs and turned toward me slightly, in the finishing school manner. Not long after I had seated myself, she again fixed on me with that penetrating look. "You're safe!" she said. "I know, for I have checked. Other clergy spouses have told me, 'He is safe.'" I had not heard that comment so precisely before. It was a dramatic clue to what was coming.

After some moments of silence, she relaxed her gaze and said, "Let me tell you about myself." Here were more indicators of a sophisticated woman with ego resources, and ready to do the serious work of psychotherapy.

"I'm a rich bitch," she said matter-of-factly. "And I have a deep, dark secret. I've been working on it for some years now, with a pastor and a psychiatrist. The pastor helped me discover that I had this deep secret, and that my spiritual confusion was likely a consequence. The psychiatrist taught me how to take pills to feel better. They both set me up with seeming kindness, then raped me. I was too confused to resist."

She took a deep breath, settled back in the chair, closed her eyes, and was silent. Shortly after, I noticed the tears begin to run down her cheeks. The tears were followed by silent, shaking sobs. Soon handfuls of tissues were needed.

I was surprised by how silently she sobbed. Yet there was a message in this also.

When she was able to speak with a measure of control, she said, "It hurts, terribly!"

"But at least I know what's wrong . . . terribly wrong."

A series of appointments followed. She had to tell me about the "deep, dark secret," but only after a serial recitation of the abuses by the psychiatrist and the pastor, in turn. It sometimes seemed like peeling back the layers of an onion. In each appointment it was important for her to spend part of the time telling about the good things she was doing with her life, and how she was going to take care of herself the following week, in order to sustain health as she worked through the ordeal of memories.

The good information she shared was about a privileged childhood and adolescence, living with an older brother and younger sister on an island estate, and attending private schools. Though her father was preoccupied and emotionally distant, she knew he was proud of her achievements. Her mother provided warm intimacy, and her nannies hovered around her through grade school.

After an Ivy League education, she married a promising young pastor, whose church career thrived, and often kept him away from the lovely home given them by her parents. She had spent much of her adulthood raising two sons and being active in prestigious women's organizations and charitable activities.

The tragic information included the senility of her father, and the incompetence of her brother as he tried to manage the family estate. More importantly, the shadowy figure of an uncle, who was a pastor, emerged from her buried memories. He had been a frequent visitor at the family estate when she was growing up. After some probing counseling with the pastor who first counseled her, she began to remember that this uncle often came to her bedroom in secret and indulged in what he told her were "love matches." They would roll around on her bed playfully, then he would undress and fondle her. As she developed, he began to have sexual intercourse with her. She didn't understand this, but since he was careful not to hurt her, she thought this must be the love he mentioned. This routine continued over several years, and though she reported she felt uneasy about the secrecy as well as the behavior, she never told anyone. But when she went to college, she learned from other girls more about what had happened with her uncle. A couple of her friends had had similar experiences, and spoke of this with the shame and confusion she was beginning to feel. After her marriage, she found herself becoming more and more depressed.

The depression didn't fit her understanding of her religious faith. So she decided to talk to one of the pastors at her church, whom she liked. She began to meet with him regularly, since he had training in counseling. During these sessions they probed her childhood and slowly uncovered the haunting sexual abuse by her uncle. As her repressed emotions emerged, this pastor was solicitous, and in her feelings of appreciation she let him begin sexual abuses. Her depression returned, and the pastor referred her to a psychiatrist who provided antidepressant medication. This eased the depression, until during one of the appointments with the psychiatrist he made sexual advances. As he had intercourse with her, he said he thought it would help her deal with the now painful memories of her uncle's abuses if she had a good sexual experience with a psychiatrist.

After that episode she became panicky. It seemed that her whole world now revolved around a series of confusing and frightening sexual encounters. About this time she began charitable support for an organization devoted to caring for abused women. After hearing only a few of their dismaying stories, she became conscious of rising anger. When she heard of our pastoral counseling office from another clergy spouse, she made the appointment that began this latest desperate quest for answers and health.

Despite her cultured aplomb, I recognized the panic and depression early, and referred her to our consulting psychiatrist for appropriate medication. With this biochemical assistance, and her willingness to follow a careful exercise and health regimen, we began a lengthy process of discovery and recovery. Several years later we moved toward termination with less frequent appointments, but a continuation of regular meetings with her support group.

A few years later I felt a tap on my shoulder during a break in activities at a professional counselors conference. When I turned, she smiled and we hugged. Over coffee we caught up on the news of her progress toward an MBA, with which she intends to become the director of a growing support organization for abused women.

She reported, "The scar is still there. But I am turning it into healthy muscle!"

The Congregation as Client: A Stunned Congregation

I returned home from doing a seminar for clergy in a distant city to find an urgent message asking me to phone a denominational executive. I did so and heard a desperate plea from the executive who knew of my work. She asked me to consider serving as an interim pastor for six months at a church in which the pastor had to be removed, due to strong allegations of sexual misconduct in the town where this church was located. This executive said she and her crisis team would take care of worship and hold an informational congregational meeting at the church the next Sunday, but since it was Lenten season, her staff and reliable retired pastors were already booked. Would I please consider serving as interim pastor through Easter, and hopefully through Memorial Day, since it would take that long to arrange for an experienced pastor to serve while a pulpit search committee was formed and called a new pastor. I told her that I would spend that evening seeing if I could rearrange some schedule conflicts and praying for guidance, then phone her in the morning.

I made a commitment through Memorial Day. Two Sundays before Easter I was in the pulpit of this historic small church in a small town in the rural Midwest. I had agreed to be in the town Friday through Sunday each week. A member of the denomination's executive staff was present to introduce me. I had never been in this church before and knew only a couple of members casually, having met them at denominational events. I had asked them to have lunch with me following worship. And I spoke with the Stated Clerk of the Session (it was a Presbyterian congregation) and asked her to call a congregational meeting that Sunday afternoon, and a meeting of the Session (official board) the following Monday evening. (Events can move fast in a small town.)

I learned that this was a normal congregation with a long history. The first Sunday morning that I preached, there were sullen and tense faces in the congregation. After worship, at lunch with the two casual friends, I appealed to them to give me some honest insights into the congregation's recent history, who the official and unofficial leaders were, and what the members they knew were saying about the pastor's removal.

At the open congregational meeting, I repeated the information that I had been told concerning the removal of the pastor. Then we had a time for voluntary, spoken prayers. In those prayers I heard clues about reactions, their fears, their confusion and anger, and some anxious prayers for the future. A couple of persons prayed for the pastor and his family. No one mentioned victims. A question period followed in which I explained why and how a pastor is removed, and what happens after that. Some angry and threatening questions caused a stir for a while. Then came some caring offers to help with church tasks. This helped calm the situation.

I finally asked a pointed question: had anyone in this congregation been sexually abused by the removed pastor? A long, embarrassed but concerned silence followed. Some familiar questions followed: "Is this sort of thing happening in many churches?" "What kind of sex are we talking about here?" "What happens to the victims of such abuse?" "Can we ever trust a pastor again?" No one indicated being or knowing a victim of this pastor's sexual offenses. This, of course, is an indication that this congregation was itself one of the victims in this sexual abuse.

As emotions settled, I asked about the church's youth group, and suggested that the young people become a major focus of concern and care. Several parents asked if I would meet with their children if they brought them to church that evening. I said I was very anxious to be there, if they would do the phone work, provide the pizza, and be there themselves. Suddenly there was a spontaneous surge of energy to organize a pizza meeting at church that evening. I was told their youth had not been active in the church for several months. This turned out to be a welcome though anxious gathering.

That evening we had about a dozen kids at church, about equal numbers of girls and boys, and half a dozen parents. The young people were restless and somewhat embarrassed to be there, but they relaxed when the pizzas arrived. There was typical frivolity among the kids, and quiet conversation among parents, until the Stated Clerk of Session, whom I had asked to open the meeting, called the gathering together for an opening prayer. After she introduced me, I explained why I was there, what had happened to the pastor, and why it was important for young people to talk about sexuality and the sexual misconduct that had occurred in this congregation. Then I read the Bible story of David and Bathsheba and commented briefly, before asking what they were thinking about and what questions they had. There were both naïve and thoughtful questions. One girl asked what the church was doing about date-rape, teen pregnancy, and sexually trans- mitted diseases. No one asked about the pastor or victims. An intense, open question-and-answer session followed. A boy who was obviously a leader said, "It's about time we had meetings like this in the church."

I asked if they would like to start the youth group again, every Sunday evening. The response was enthusiastic. One girl asked if they could bring friends who were not members of this church. That led to a discussion of youth groups at other churches. One of the parents noted that the high school principal and a physician who was also a member of Kiwanis had engaged a well-known young couple, both of whom had HIV-AIDS, for an open commu- nity gathering the Sunday evening after Easter. Both youth and parents decided to talk this up to friends and other parents. They agreed to attend this meeting as a group from this church. The Sunday evening after Easter, an overflow crowd gathered in the largest church meeting space in town, the Lutheran church's ornate sanctuary. The presentation and question-and-answer time were dramatically open and successful. The whole subject of sex- uality and its misuse had been opened up in the community, with school, medical, and church sponsorship.

I had made a point of visiting with other pastors at their churches soon after my ministry here began. We discussed the issues of clergy sexual misconduct, and the issues of sexuality the young people were raising so enthusiastically. Two more ecumeni- cal, community meetings were planned, to include instructive video presentations, and brief presentations by a couple of pas- tors, the school principal, the resident physician, and a business leader. The biggest surprise came as two local young people, a girl and a boy, volunteered to speak at the meetings regarding youth problems with sexuality. The weekly county newspaper took up the cause, and this helped these "town meetings" be successful.

Sundays at this church took on a familiar pattern. There was a worship service, with my sermons directed to Scripture and themes relevant to spiritual and sexual healthiness, spiritual leadership and its problems, and celebrations of how the gospel can guide us as we deal with both the joys and the sins of human sexuality. The high-school-age Sunday School class, which was taught by a church member who was a high school teacher and myself, was very well attended. This led to an informal but focused confirmation class. A moving confirmation graduation occurred at a later Sunday worship service, in which youth confirmed their baptismal vows, and elders of the congregation laid hands on their heads and prayed for them.

Every other Sunday afternoon an open congregational meeting was held, which included prayers for the departed pastor and family, victims of sexual abuse (rumors were flying, and the school nurse was organizing a support group focused on domestic violence), and congregational marital and sexuality issues. Once a month, an informal healing service was held, following these church gatherings.

The door of congregational awareness was opening, and the responses were both painful and supportive. When my service as interim ended, an experienced pastor, suggested by the denomination, and approved by the Session and congregation, served ably as the congregation went through the process of calling a new pastor.

These three cases, along with the others in this book, provide opportunities for all of us to grow intentionally in our understanding of the perpetrators and victims of clergy sexual misconduct. This is discouraging work at the present time, for organized religion has only begun to understand the scope of its problems with sexuality, especially among its leaders. On the other hand, as one who has ministered long enough to be involved in all aspects of the sexual revolution, and in organized religion's discovery of sexual misconduct, I see and feel great thankfulness for significant progress. A major task now is sorting through all the media reports, personal stories, and research to find practical guidelines that can help us discern God's purposes for interdicting boundary violations, and supporting victims as they become healthy survivors. I begin with definitions.

Definitions

Perpetrator. This is an ominous term applied to a person who has abused or is abusing other persons sexually. It does not sound like a religious term, for we are not accustomed to discussing the dark side of sexuality in the church. We must learn quickly that perpetrators of sexual abuse are often church members, sometimes clergy, whose personal lives include serious sexual misconduct. They are human beings, many of them believers. Their religious faith and their sexuality have become disconnected. Terms such as abuser, offender, violator, batterer, rapist, and predator are somewhat synonymous, although each may indicate some specific misconduct.

Victim-survivor. Victims are persons who have been abused and are not fully recovered. Survivors are victims who are recovering and building relatively normal lives. These terms are often used together in this book, to indicate the reality that most victims survive in some relatively functional condition, with or without specialized assistance. Too many do not. It is very important that the church be actively and competently involved in ministries focused toward all victims, so they may become healthy survivors. "Victim" is a forbidding and empty word, unless it touches our hearts. Listing some of the powerful emotions and characteristics common to victims may help.

Captive. Children, women, and men who have been traumatically abused often experience a preconscious or conscious feeling of being captive to the power of the abuser. Thus, they are afraid to do anything to anger their "captor." The feeling of being captive remains until they believe they are free to live in safety. Long-term consequences for many abused girls and young women is predictably bleak. Nonetheless, there is hope in Sandra Knauer's book, *Recovering from Sexual Abuse, Addictions, and Compulsive Behaviors* (2002). She warns, "The female survivor quickly learns that to be female is to be under someone else's control. Such female survivors grow up never knowing their own sense of power" (288).

Confused. Confusion is a most common part of a victim's reactions to being abused. Normal assumptions, self-concept, confidence in spiritual leaders, and trust in God's justice are all distorted by sexual violation.

Shamed. The human experience of shame is much more than shyness or guilt or the typical childhood experience of being teased by peers, feeling embarrassed in public, or having one's genitals exposed. Shame is learned by seeing adult responses to certain situations, by comparing oneself to peers, or by feeling exposed and vulnerable, or by having one's body abused in secret. With long exposure to experiences of shame or in having a degrading traumatic experience, shame becomes part of a person's self-concept. Shame undercuts personal confidence and normal assertiveness, leaving passive inferiority, or vengeful outbursts as responses to threat or public scrutiny. Shame, when connected to normal sexual encounters, leaves the victim unable to trust a partner or believe in personal worth and attractiveness. This broad perspective on human shame is discussed by Karen A. McClintock (2001).

Rage. Anger is a normal human response, and a marker on the "identity agenda" of human emotions (see "Agendas for Human Behavior," chapter 8, below). Anger is a natural response to personal violations and disrespect. When the violation is traumatic, either in emotional impact or extended duration, however, normal anger is intensified by shock, pain, and fear. A sexually violated person is often an enraged person and therefore capable of violent responses to threatening behavior or the presence of an abuser. Rational behavior may not be possible without assistance.

Connected. This is one name for the experience of solidarity born of common experience and hopes. It includes the relief and reassurance of not being alone, and the synergy of persons with similar concerns. Victims of sexual abuse often find this experience in small groups of victims who also were abused. Christie Cozad Neuger (2001) develops the concept of connectedness as a key to victims becoming survivors. She teaches the steps needed: telling and clarifying the personal story, dealing with depression, learning to make choices, and staying connected with other women. Her book, *Counseling Women,* offers therapeutic insights and methods for assisting in the healing of abused women.

Empowered. This designates the sense of liberation, recovery, and clarity of mission experienced by victims of sexual abuse, when in a recovery mode, and guided by a sense of personal potency and worthwhile goals. Empowerment is often a function of the connectedness described above.

Each person's experience of victimhood is unique in some ways. Further, there are gender differences. For example, when boys are sexually violated, they often experience severe shame and humiliation in their undeveloped maleness. They then are imprinted with a negative model of male sexuality and love. And they are likely to distrust adult males, unless they in desperation bond with one who offers them succor. Adult males are likely to experience sexual abuse as a humiliating loss of male confidence. They then become inappropriately abusive or passively dependent. Girls are likely to feel shamed and damaged in femininity and thereafter distrustful of adult males. Women often feel permanently blemished and inferior along with characteristics mentioned above.

Professional boundary. This is a limitation placed on professional behavior by a certifying (ordaining) organization through its code of ethics/behavior, its disciplines, and as interpreted by a legal system empowered to sit in judgment. Boundaries, as the term is used in regard to sexual misconduct, is also a preconscious assumption by potential victims. Nearly all persons in our society have a sense of acceptable behavior by professionals, especially in relationship to personal and mental safety. When a perpetrator violates such boundaries, trust, respect, and self-confidence are lost. Therefore, professional boundaries for clergy must now be clear and enforced, in order to clarify traditional behavioral standards, to offer safety to vulnerable persons, and to remain compliant before civil and criminal laws. Boundaries exist also in all the helping professions, which though not officially inscribed, are valuable resources based on common sense, good judgment, respect and caring, and on contextual insights.

Vulnerability/at risk. Vulnerability, as used in relationship to professional interaction with clients, describes a client, supplicant, or person present with few resources for self-protection. *At risk*, as used here, means a professional helper, boss, or guide who by misbehavior or poor judgment can damage or harm a person(s), including herself, within the sphere of her or his superior competence or responsibility.

Power/control. Defining these terms is perilous when they are applied to clergy sexual misconduct, for they are subject to biases, prejudices, misinformation, and tunnel vision. The professional "authority" of clergy is an example of such peril. If all sexual misconduct is attributed to the power and control of a pastor in relationship to a parishioner or subordinate, a duality of perception, responsibility, and experience is imposed. If power and control are attributed to the pastoral role, an assumption regarding God's implication is involved. Then if the reciprocal power of the parishioner to react in overpowering ways, or the congregation and denomination to apply discipline, is ignored, we no longer have justice. And, most importantly, in contemporary religious experiences, if the pastor doesn't understand the mystical, psychological, and professional power to manipulate and abuse a parishioner, he or she is not a true or faithful pastor.

Forgiveness/reconciliation. These are sensitive words for victim-survivors. For the religious traditions of forgiveness often presume an easier process than reality allows. If forgiveness is to occur, it must be on the victim's terms. For the sexual abuse occurred on the offender's terms. Many recent books describe the anguished and courageous path victims follow in trying to recover and forgive. (If this is not a familiar issue, check Morris 1998 and Cooper-White 1995.)

Reconciliation is even more difficult. Often it is not possible without renewing the abuse and suffering. Our religious traditions idealize both forgiveness and reconciliation. These are indeed worthy goals. Yet the experience of victims tells us we must be supportive and patient, and share God's grace as it helps bridge the chasms between trauma and forgiveness.

Dietrich Bonhoeffer's well-known warning against "cheap grace" in *The Cost of Discipleship* is helpful. "Cheap grace is the preaching of forgiveness without requiring repentance. . . . Costly grace . . . must be sought again and again. . . . Costly grace is the incarnation of God" (cited by Cooper-White 1995, p. 253).

The five steps of the traditional Christian theology of forgiveness are based upon the assumption of normally functioning, rational persons. Therefore, the first step, hearing the gospel of forgiveness, depends on hearing in a life situation where all persons involved in an offense are free to act on its message. In sexual misconduct, however, the offender has already offended and may do so again. And the victim's experience of justice is already violated and distorted by fear. The second step, confessing our sin, implies that each person realizes their sin and is contrite. Abusers often are not contrite, while victims may be willing to assume guilt for the abuse. The third step, receiving forgiveness, may be "cheap grace" for the offender, while the victim, in the confusion of the boundary violation, does not feel either forgiven or ready to offer forgiveness. The fourth step, making restitution, seems nearly impossible. The offender cannot give back what was stolen. The victim does not know what a just compensation can be. The fifth step, pronouncing absolution, may again be "cheap grace" for the offender. And the victim will typically be unwilling, or in no condition to give closure, and accept reconciliation. The theologies of organized religion must develop forgiveness-reconciliation practices that include justice and patience with the victim's recovery.

Addiction. This term is both a clinical and judgmental term in our society. It can be related to a biochemical or genetic factor or develop out of an obsessive habit of overindulgence with a substance or experience that alters consciousness substantially. In the relational sense, it can mean a habitual dependence on an experience, relationship, or fantasy that interferes with healthy thinking and behavior. For example, a person can become addicted to a co-dependent relationship (both or all persons involved will be addicted), to a version of religion, or to an imagined scenario in which certain behavior or experience must be had for security. The term is used or implied with both meanings here. We must be alert to the dangers in deeming all or most sexual misconduct as a function of addiction. For such a perspective allows for the disease model to usurp causal responsibility and imply an unrealistic role for those treating or managing the person afflicted. Further, it now implies an overreaching recommendation for therapy based on a Twelve-Step recovery model, to the exclusion of other proven therapies.

Spiritual warfare. Although this term is not used often in this book, it is an important assumption. The term has been applied excessively to unwanted or misunderstood conflict or behavior. Yet it is a real dynamic in all of creation, as far as we know, since the beginning of time. As used here, it means the ancient conflict between good and evil. In this usage it implies that spiritual forces influence human behavior, and sometimes determine it. But it does not imply superstition nor little green imps nor demon possession. It does mean, however, that persons, groups, and organizations can give themselves to evil intentions and behavior, temporarily or long-term. Thus, the familiar terminology of salvation and conversion can have therapeutic and grace-filled meanings and applications when applied with discernment.

  Sex therapist. This term must be included here, even though it is not discussed in this book. A sex therapist is an officially designated professional (educators, clergy, therapists, medical professionals, marriage counselors) with specialized training in human sexuality and related issues. When planning rehabilitation of clergy engaged in unhealthy sex or offenses, the therapy should include persons with this designation. Some types of counselors imagine themselves to be competent in sex therapy but are not. In our puritanical and judgmental society (especially including organized religion), even professional helpers usually have limiting sexual biases and are therefore incompetent to analyze and treat sexual dysfunction. The website http://www.aasect.org/Home (key word: sex therapist) lists religiously oriented as well as secular sites and organizations.

Therapeutic Models and Interventions

For Individuals

  Cognitive-behavioral therapy. This model uses either cognitive therapies (probing, evaluating, guidance/advice, reframing, meditation) or behavioral therapies (changing behaviors and habits) to clarify abuse, responsibility, and options for recovery. This therapeutic modality is replacing Analytic-Insight Therapy, which may be somewhat more thorough but is expensive and long-term.

Medical treatment. This model uses prescriptive drugs, such as antiandrogens (Depo-Provera, et al.) and agonists (Lupron), to override the sexual excitations and male characteristics of androgens (testosterone, androsterone) and thus lessen sexual desire and aggression. Antidepressants are used to lessen anxiety and depression and to quiet obsessive-compulsive tendencies. These treatments are used in conjunction with talk and behavioral therapies, sometimes as out-patient treatments, and often as in-patient modalities, in treatment centers such as St. Luke Institute, Silver Spring, Maryland. This is the treatment of choice for pedophiles, rapists, and some batterers.

Group therapy. This is a popular, relatively inexpensive, easy-to-manage, and effective modality for offenders not limited by mental impairment, are non-addictive, and not afflicted with personality disorders. It can be used to teach, evaluate, modify nonpsychotic disorders, support cognitive and behavioral change, and generate spiritual nurture. This modality's effectiveness is enhanced significantly when combined with individual or marital therapy. It is quite effective in use with troubled congregations.

Addiction therapy. Essentially modeled on the Alcoholics Anonymous Twelve-Step recovery plan, it is highly effective in treating substance abuse and dysfunction related to behavior intended for excessive comfort or pleasure. It is offered in modified regimens to bring "sobriety" to those addicted to a relationship (co-dependency), to fantasy experiences (video games, etc.), to a religion or an organized ideology, or to an experience (the "highs" and escapism) of such activities as distance running, watching TV, etc.). It was designed for and is most effective in treating substance abuses (alcohol, drugs, foodstuffs). More recently it has been effective in treating obsessive-compulsive syndromes and the excesses of porno-masturbation and the "virtual sex" of cybersex. For all its effectiveness with substance abuse and some obsessive-compulsive behavior, it should not be presumed effective nor the primary modality for interdicting all undesirable behavior.

Spiritual direction. This historic, and now revived, modality is quite effective for spiritual nurture, behavioral guidance, and moral transformations where traditional spirituality is ego-syntonic. It is valuable in treating many sexual disorders and victim syndromes when combined with individual therapy.

Exercise therapy and massage therapy. There is growing evidence that disciplined exercise (regular, interesting, goal-oriented), and healing hands massage (deep tissue, cranial-sacral, Reiki, and others), enhance most therapeutic modalities. Lifestyles that include these are less prone to stress, abuse, and addiction.

Post-traumatic stress disorder (PTSD). This perspective on sexual abuse and trauma is based upon the experiences of terror, violence, and shocking abuse during World War II and the Vietnam War, and refined further in dealing with similar terrorizing emergencies and abuses across the U.S. It indicates that a deeply shocking and abusive event or experience leaves permanent distortions of perception and reaction to danger. The memories of such events triggers a nonrational reaction of fear, flashback memories, avoidance behavior, and depression. Sexual abuse may wound a victim's psyche deeply enough to cause this syndrome. Effective treatment includes individual psychotherapy, antidepressant/antianxiety medications, and continuing support group involvement. Cure may not be possible, but rehabilitation is.

Intervention. This modality can be effective with individuals, groups, or organizations that have become dysfunctional. Essentially it is an intentional, assertive, and focused interdiction of inappropriate or potentially damaging conduct in an effort to end unwanted behavior and consequences. In the Bible we have examples, sometimes called "exorcism" (Mark 5), and in the Catholic tradition there exists a ritual for ending demon possession. An intervention protocol is now used commonly by religious organizations to manage the complexities of removing a sexually offending pastor from the parish of his/her service. It often has variations suited to denominational theology, polity, and legal guidelines, and typically is informed by psychological insights concerning its applications. In order to be effective, a therapeutic intervention must be carried out with enough authority, resolve, and planning to assure its effectiveness. An intervention in organized religion is ordinarily initiated on orders from a top executive, an empowered task force, or a team of professionals or trained lay persons. It should not be attempted by a lone individual or in the absence of a tested plan.

For Groups

Family therapy is now a well-established therapeutic modality. Many mental health professionals are trained in it. Individual therapists are not typically effective in dealing with traumatized families. The families of victims and offenders should be referred to therapeutic teams trained in family therapy.

Congregational therapy is not a distinct modality. It is being developed now on a trial-and-error basis. So far, a relatively effective protocol consists of informational meetings for congregations, followed by sermons on relevant topics, small groups convened around relevant issues, support groups, and individual therapeutic consultations for deeply troubled persons. Prayer and meditation events are ego-syntonic and welcome. Healing services are valuable later, when victims and troubled persons become known.

We can apply these definitions, characteristics, and therapeutic strategies with some generic, brief guidance from the following protocols. Many denominational offices and congregations now have a plan for such applications. It is valuable to develop a plan that fits local conditions.

Applications

Part I

1. **Assessment and diagnosis are crucial.** There should be an emergency plan written somewhere. Find it and follow it. Assessment can be done by knowledgeable, caring leaders. First stop the bleeding. Then comes an eyes-open, prayerful inspection of the scene, persons, and resources. Now discerning decisions can be made. Diagnosis should be done by specialized professionals. It is not helpful to attempt therapy until you understand what is wrong.

2. **Care of victims must begin immediately.**
- Identify victims. Provide safety and care. Assess what is needed.
- Notify law enforcement authorities if a minor is involved.
- Prepare relevant information for "Need to Know" persons.
- Communicate with all involved—carefully. Keep records.
- Provide for congregational needs. Support family/spouse/partner appropriately.

3. **Care of perpetrator follows.**
- Separate perpetrator(s) from the scene and from victims.
- Establish communication; if perpetrator has fled, search.
- Arrange safety and therapy.

4. **Short-term recovery follows.**
- There should be a short-range plan written somewhere. Find it and follow it.

This is a brief outline of the steps for management of clergy sexual misconduct as it is discovered. Congregations and denominational offices should have a guidebook easily available that is based upon their polity and local legal mandates. For it is as vital as a first-aid kit with instructions. Mistakes made in emergencies are costly.

Part II

Debrief the current situation.
- Evaluate the written plans for such situations. Did they work?
- Review the Part I process.
- Gather information as needed.
- What happened? What went wrong, and right?
- Establish long-term care for victims (specialists and congregation).
- Review the legal factors (insurance, lawyers, official communications). Christian Ministries Resources is a fine source of legal guidance. They publish a newsletter analyzing court cases relevant to church issues: "Church Law and Tax Report" (phone number is 704-821-3845; website is www.churchlawtoday.com).
- Evaluate the professional diagnosis of the perpetrator. How does this guide us? What therapy and care must be provided?

Part III

Establish a long-term plan.
- There should be a long-term plan written somewhere. Find it and follow it.
- Sustain the recovery process.
- Plan the new normalcy. Seek a God-given vision for the future.

Part IV

Develop health and fitness.
- There probably is no written plan yet for health and fitness. Write one.

Much of the planning in denominational offices and elsewhere is focused on crisis-management. Some denominational offices also have codes of conduct and strategies for training. A plan for prevention and for developing healthy pastors and congregations is also needed. Interventions, though painful, are opportunities for revitalization. But such opportunities must be guided and reinforced competently.

Prevention

Here is a definition of prevention by acronym:

P = Preparation. Many denominational offices and executives have codes of conduct, along with training in this code for staff, pastors, and lay leaders. The preparations should include guidelines for prevention specifically applicable to congregations. The congregation must have a primary role in prevention of sexual misconduct by all staff, volunteers and members. The best prevention strategy is to focus on the body-mind-spirit health of the congregation and its leaders. Health is as contagious as sickness.

R = Regularity. Systematic planning and disciplines are not typical for many congregations, pastors, and denominational offices. There may be weekly schedules, but preventative regularity means establishing an effective discipline and accountability pattern that will hold the community of faith in healthy lifestyles and mission.

E = Evaluation. In our age of transitions, health is sustained through continual monitoring of procedures, accountability safeguards, and lifestyles. What seemed like a good idea last year may not be viable today.

V = Values. In an era of easy morals and confused theology, all members of the community share responsibility to learn again how God intended for us to live: how can we care for each other, lift the oppressed, and value this planet? Doctrines and creeds can be helpful, but it is a spiritually disciplined and active valuing process that keeps a community of faith and its leaders healthy.

E = Excellence. Perfection is not a realistic goal for the prevention of sexual misconduct. God calls us to be the best that we can be. Business-as-usual is not adequate. When we keep calling each other to excellence, we find that health (realistic excellence) is joyful and satisfying.

N = Network. The story of a pastor-congregation too healthy for sexual misconduct is a story of healthy relationships. The three key words in a healthy community of faith are: relationships . . . relationships . . . relationships; all healthy connections.

T = Terror. We are learning again the power of fear. Terror is fear out of control. Yet fear can be valuable in preserving life and avoiding abuse. Healthy fear of consequences is a powerful motivation for healthy living and for the prevention of sexual misconduct. The biblical guideline is "The fear of the Lord is the beginning of wisdom" (Proverbs 9:10).

Training and Accountability

Training is the guided learning of health and spiritual growth, and the discipline of preventing sickness and spiritual death. Without disciplined training the community of faith is left floundering, as was Israel without healthy leaders and training in faith: "Everyone did what was right in his own eyes" (Judges 21:25).

Accountability is the monitored stewardship of behavior and resources. The legal system has demonstrated that if organized religion will not discipline itself appropriately, the courts will. Learning to respect each other and the laws of spiritual health works better.

Study Exercise

To make the definitions and therapy descriptions clearer, write your own definitions of the terms, and your own perspectives on how each therapy modality would work in cases you know.

To analyze the stories, think of what would happen if the offender and the victim-survivor talked together.

To study the intervention applications, compare this generic summary with the sexual crisis policies operant in your denomination.

Summary

This chapter urges serious attention to the dark side of religion. When we are honest about some of the consequences of our business-as-usual perspectives and hear the anguish of victims, we can focus on the true priorities of ministry.

Three stories are presented to highlight the plight of victims of clergy sexual misconduct done to a boy, a woman, and a congregation. They represent many who are not yet heard or healed.

In response to the anguish of victims, and with our courageous and anxious efforts to heal and prevent further devastation, guiding summaries are presented. This summarizing began with definitions of relevant terms. Then come summaries of therapeutic modalities and interventions, with a generic model for intervention. It is important for all of us to share in the healing.

Part Three
Healthy Sexuality

8. WHY PEOPLE ACT AS THEY DO

STOP, TAKE A DEEP BREATH, and turn away from the sordid world of abusive, insidious, and dissonant sexuality in previous chapters. Why have these two waves of sexual revolution occurred? Did our genes change? No. Did our hormones change? No. Did the environment change? Yes, socially and materially. Socially, capitalistic democracy grew out of and produced more individualism. Materially, the industrialized world began to see what nature-oriented societies already knew, namely, that the environment mirrors the effects of human behavior. Individualism drew us toward quick gratification of personal needs, with little regard for long-term effects. The human tendency toward altruism is not strong enough to offset individualism without continual reinforcement. Such powerful and continuous trends help make sexual activity attractive and easily manipulated.

To help us understand the phenomena of distorted sexuality, we will consider two general perspectives on why people act as they do. This chapter gives a broad perspective on human motivation by reviewing the psychology of human behavior and then by examining the way we organize our behavior through ethics.

Human behavior is both mystifying and transparent. One day we think, "I can read him like a book." Another time we can hardly believe what she is doing. This is true of sexual misconduct in the church. For when we know the warning signals—and *believe* what we see—sexual misconduct can be visible, predictable, and preventable. When we ask, "How in God's name (clergy, remember?) could he do such a thing—and without us knowing," there is an answer. We can know, if we choose to.

Information about why people act as they do can aid us as we try to discern the prescriptions our Creator has already written for sin and evil. It is sometimes difficult to understand sin and evil actions when they are perpetrated by pastors who seem normal. The following schema, agendas for human behavior, will give clues about the stresses and motivations of sexual offenders. And it can guide our efforts to understand, to discipline, to care and heal, to prevent, and to grow toward the healthy sexuality God intends for us and for creation.

The most basic information we need is an understanding of motivations, the engines that drive our behavior at a primal, unconscious level. For human sexuality is a drive, a basic urge, one of the most potent of human incentives. And when its powerful hormones are in service to one of the following agendas, we might have a sexuality of fear or of pleasure, anger, love, sadness, or joy. Understanding these possible connections makes it easier to manage both distorted and healthy impulses and behavior.

The following schema is a theoretical construct that has its roots in the teachings of Sigmund Freud, Carl Jung, Virginia Satir, Heinz Kohut, Abraham Maslow, and others; in the tripartite brain model developed by Paul MacLean at the National Institute of Mental Health (1984); and in John Ratey's research on the brain (2001). I developed this model to aid pastors in understanding motivations and behaviors, in themselves and in their parishioners, and offer it here to aid in connecting the sexual issues we are studying with everyday physical-mental-spiritual experiences. Please refer to the legend below for an explanation of the schema's structure.

Agendas for Human Behavior

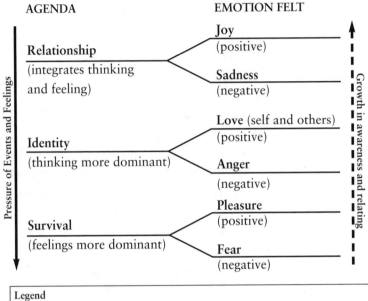

Legend
Agenda = primary, overriding motivation pattern
Emotion = a set of feelings that induce physiological change and behavior
Solid arrow = Downward pressure of events and feelings
Dotted arrow = Growth in awareness, self-management skills, and caring
"Negative" and "positive" do not denote good and bad but a flow of energy in the polarity of two potent emotions

Agendas for Human Behavior

Each of the following three agendas is organized around a polarity of identifying emotions so strong that this agenda overrules others when it becomes the chosen motivation in a person's life, temporarily or long-term. Stimuli and suggestions not compatible with this motivation are screened out. Any conversation, experience, or idea that does not fit the dominating agenda receives little conscious attention.

Much of this motivational process is generated in our unconscious mind. The *survival agenda* is essentially a function of the reptilian brain, the primitive brain-stem area. This is much like the brain of reptiles, which is reactive rather than cognitive. It determines behavior in response to environmental and internal cues. There is minimal self-insight on the survival identity—only the awarenesses that facilitate survival.

The *identity agenda* is generated by the limbic system, the middle area of the brain that we have in common with mammals. This area of our brains becomes dominant when no threats to survival are perceived. With the limbic system we have emotions and feelings, some memory, and many of our personality traits. Although habits and unconscious cues generate some behavior on this agenda, much self-awareness is involved.

On the *relationship agenda* the neocortex is dominant. Here memory, rationality, and awareness of the feelings and emotions of other persons work together to guide behavior.

Survival Agenda

Survival agenda sounds negative, even frightening. It is primitive, but it is also basic. Although this is an agenda for the animal part of us, it can be lived in a civilized way, as most of us do. The focused questions that dominate this agenda are: Am I safe here? Will I survive? Trying to survive and to be comfortable are the powerful motivations that drive this agenda. The identifying law is the "law of the jungle"—"kill or be killed," "an eye for an eye"). The identifying emotions are fear and pleasure (the energy polarity).

The survival agenda is not all negative and reactive. Many people get stuck on it. In fact, it is our normal agenda, the one with which we are born. But it is a very limiting agenda. When we live on it continuously there is little energy available for creativity, growth, and intimacy. The great detriment in this agenda is the predominance of fear (anxiety) and its polar opposite, pleasure-seeking (stress reduction), to relieve the constant anxiety.

Persons on this agenda tend to think defensively, in either/or terms, and to resist change unless it offers an obvious aid to their survival and pleasure. Extroverted types will be belligerent or defensive. Introverted types will be quiet and stubborn. Survivors relate readily to those they perceive as allies and resist persons they perceive as enemies or prey. They will attack or resist with ferocity and tenacity, as jungle animals do with enemies. Their lives will be organized around protective rituals. Their coping mechanisms or stress reducers will focus on comforting, pleasurable activities, and sensual materials. They tend to interpret communication with others in terms of threats or reassurance. If they perceive assurance of safety, they can move to a higher agenda.

The behavior of persons who function on the survival agenda will exhibit the effects of fear and pleasure seeking—the most powerful of human emotions. Neither of the other agendas can match the emotional power of this one. This agenda is triggered whenever there is disruption, significant change, or some strong precipitating experience (flashbacks, injuries, seduction). Persons on this agenda respond readily to other persons sharing this agenda, if this does not pose a threat. Behavior may be crude and obvious or sophisticated and subtle. Many nice, normal people never get beyond this agenda in their lives. Many mentally disordered persons are limited to the gross or violent versions. Comfort and security are critical to the positive management of this agenda.

Since the basic needs of this agenda are safety, nurture, freedom, and pleasure, intimacy at this level means a relationship that meets these needs in some way. Arguing or trying to change a survivor's mind will be fruitless. But offering reassuring materials and rituals can modify behavior. Acceptable activities (private or shared) will feature physical activity, expressions of bravado, sensual pleasures, nest building, and rituals celebrating security. When the identifying question of this survival agenda (Am I safe here?) has been answered adequately, we are able to move up to the next higher agenda.

Before moving to the next higher agenda, an application is valuable. Have you noticed the likely flow of energy (attention, compulsion) between the emotions (poles) that govern this agenda? When deeply afraid (anxiety), a person soon seeks relief from the tension fear produces. The most natural reaction is to relieve this stress with quick, readily available stress reducers (alcohol, junk food, escapism, and sex instead of deep breathing, exercise, and wise decisions). If a person is already caught in an addiction or counterproductive habit pattern when fear strikes, the addiction takes control with a reassurance of temporary relief of the tension. If the addiction is cybersex, for example, all that's needed is a computer and a little privacy. Healthier ways of managing anxiety must be firmly established in order to beat the competition of unhealthy stress reducers.

Notice also that when the fears of losing safety or comfort are triggered, the temporary pleasure and comfort of unhealthy stress reducers not only wear off but also often leave the anxieties of guilt trips, hangovers, unhealthiness, and possible consequences with victims. The pleasure principle is a poor antidote for the fears of loss, pain, failure, or sexual frustration that so often press us down to the survival agenda. Much better is a disciplined lifestyle that handles high anxiety with healthy behaviors and by eliminating the sources of anxiety. Release from the survival agenda does not come through good intentions or quick fixes. Healthy lifestyles offer the best freedom from the limitations of living with anxiety and stress reducers. When the safety and comfort question is answered satisfactorily, a person is ready to move up to the next higher agenda.

Identity Agenda

The identity agenda focuses on these questions: Who am I? What difference do I make? The identifying law is the law of competition (win-lose). The identifying emotions are anger and love (the polarity). The healthiest motivation is to be the best that I can be.

The characteristics of this agenda are similar to those of survival. But this agenda is less brutal and more socialized. Persons on this agenda are highly sensitive to their own personhood. Consciously or unconsciously, they struggle with this question: What's in it for me?

Persons on this agenda tend to think in terms of life as a stage drama with themselves as a central character. They compare themselves to others if they are introverted types, and compare others to themselves if extroverted. Introverts will quietly watch the drama to learn and evaluate their part. Extroverts will try to shape the drama for their own benefit. Both types will be assessing the effect of their presence.

This is the agenda in which insight (the ability to see and understand ourselves) is most likely to develop. The self-centeredness of this agenda can be both positive and negative. Individuals concentrating on themselves may come to understand themselves at a deep level. They may become aware of the difference they can make in relationships and society. They often develop their behavior in ways that help others win with them. It is especially helpful to have a mentor when on this agenda, to help shape, model, and assess the developing personality.

The needs of a person on the identity agenda are for affirmation, affection, and achievement. Their primary intimate relationships, therefore, will focus on the meeting of these needs. They will be attracted, on the one hand, to persons who respond positively toward them. They will be hurt or irritated with persons who do not give them affirmation. Those who give them positive regard may be rewarded with gestures of appreciation.

The energy generated by the interaction of anger and love on this agenda can be confusing to both actor and observer. Anger, being undesirable, may be camouflaged and repressed. Love, being acceptable, is prominent, whether sincere or contrived.

Love is a learned emotion. Human beings are not born with it, as we are born with fear, pleasure seeking, and anger. We are born with only the potential for love. And this may be shaped into distortions such as aggression, seduction, and manipulation that can be mistaken for love. Children who grow up without unconditional love and models of healthy love may be unable to express positive love, even when they wish to.

We also need to remind ourselves that love is not experienced as love, no matter how sincere the intention of the giver, unless it is given in ways that are perceived as love by the receiver. We sometimes distort the true meaning of the Golden Rule when we literally try to treat others as if they felt, thought, and lived as we do. We haven't said, "I care about you," until we say it in ways that mean caring to the other person.

A person whose self-esteem is violated or abused (by their own behavior or by a partner) will likely be pushed down to the survival agenda. Enough affirmation, affection, and achievement make it possible instead for a person to move up to the highest of all the agendas.

Relationship Agenda

The identifying motivation of this agenda is to answer the question: How can we relate positively to each other, to others, and to all of creation? The identifying law is the law of buoyancy (partners will not let others sink). The identifying emotions are sadness and joy (the polarity).

This is the noblest and most tenuous of the agendas. Self-interest, danger, and social upsets tend to push persons down to the survival agenda. But the human needs for relationships and sharing impel one upward, yet with less intensity than the downward impulse. The dynamics of this agenda concentrate on common concerns and interdependence. However, the energy generated by the polarity of joy and sadness can strengthen or weaken relationships.

Persons on this agenda tend to be aware of the needs and agendas of other persons. Extroverts on this agenda will solicit feelings and needs and express their own. Introverts are patient and supportive. Both have an expanded consciousness of human feelings, behavior, shared consequences, human limits, and a sense of what is sacred.

Anxiety and distress are lessened on this agenda. The frightening survival questions and the anguished identity questions are being answered, at least temporarily. Life does not have to be managed alone. With this decrease of distress and anxiety, coping mechanisms and stress reducers are needed less. Therefore, there is energy available for caring and ministries. Individual gifts and graces become apparent and useful for all participants. Persons on this agenda do not ignore their own needs, but they have learned to meet them modestly. It is natural and satisfying for them to seek to be helpful to others and to fulfill their responsibilities in creation.

Individuals, couples, and families on this agenda do not suddenly find life easy and relationships compatible. But they waste less energy and resources on counterproductive and competitive activities.

Sadness, on the one hand, is the negative emotion that marks this agenda. There is profound pain in the loss of relationships, missed opportunities to share and understand human needs, and the destructiveness of irresponsible human behavior and thinking. This sadness promotes neither vengeance (as does anger) nor fight-flight (as does fear). It responds to human need with empathy, even though it suffers with the thought of what might have been. Apology and forgiveness are more common.

Joy is the natural, positive emotion that celebrates this agenda. It relishes responsibility (within limits), sharing (in appropriate ways), and the pleasure, love, and joy of others. Joy energizes ministries, and sadness energizes people to try again more creatively.

It is pleasant to imagine what happens to primary intimate relationships when one or both partners function on the relationship agenda, even part of the time. Individual marriage partners, couples, and families who know how to answer the needs of the lower agendas and climb to the highest agenda can spend much of their lives in peace and healthy intimacy. It is true that many of life's pressures push people downward to the survival level. But it is also true that people can learn how to move quickly up through the agendas to the highest level. This works best when it is not done alone.

Application

The three agendas apply to families, groups, and congregations as well as to individuals and couples. Complications arise when relating persons are on different agendas or are changing quickly from one agenda to another. But it is helpful to know what the agendas are and how to manage them more healthfully. (For an excellent aid in applying psychological theory and research to pastoral ministry, consult Johnson and Johnson 2000.)

1. Relationship agenda
   - Sadness: A relationship not working, a colleague self-destructing
   - Joy: Respect, synergy, creativity in relationships, collegial group succeeding in mission

2. Identity agenda
   - Anger: Furious at sexual rejection, frustrated at inability to "perform"
   - Love: Acceptance and affirmation, intimacy of affection

3. Survival agenda
   - Fear: Afraid of not getting enough sex, afraid of the consequences of sex
   - Pleasure: Euphoria of orgasm, quick release of tension

Answering the following questions may help clarify the information and import of these dominating agendas for human behavior. Do not expect easy, categorical clues from the descriptions of these agendas. The value lies in seeing tendencies and at-risk warning signs. The other factors related to sexual misconduct presented later in this chapter will also suggest some tendencies and at-risk warning signals.

1. How do you know when you are under heavy survival stress?
2. What do you do to relieve such fears?
3. How do you know when you are being disrespected?
4. What do you do when this happens?
5. How do you feel when a relationship important to you is failing?
6. What do you do about this?
7. On which of the three agendas would healthy sexuality be most difficult?
8. Where on the three agendas would each type of clergy sex offender we have discussed most likely have difficulties that could contribute to sexual offenses?

In a world of change and stability, of belief and unbelief, of sickness and health, these agendas are triggered often. It is helpful to know what agenda is driving personal thinking and behavior in any circumstance, and how to manage oneself toward more time moving upward into the relational agenda.

An Ethics of Consequences

Why people act as they do is a haunting question as we review the sexual abuses and distorted thinking by clergy who lose or never had a reliable moral-spiritual reference point. After reviewing psychological perspectives on this question in the agendas for human behavior, I turn to a contemporary perspective on social and personal ethics. In it theological morality and pragmatic ethics are conflated into an everyday philosophy of life that is particularly American.

We can call this ethical system *consequential ethics,* for its premises are based on choosing behavioral options according to the known or projected consequences with which a person wants to live. Imbedded in this ethics is a residue of the ancient struggle between two major streams of ethical thought, the absolutist (constructionist) perspectives and the pragmatic (essentialist) perspectives.

One of the classics in sociotheological ethics is H. Richard Niebuhr's *Christ and Culture* (1951). In this seminal volume he posits five major types of relationship between Christ and culture: "Christ against culture," "Christ above culture," "Christ and culture in paradox," "Christ transforming culture," and "the Christ of culture." Although this perspective leaves out a specific Jewish perspective and sounds a bit archaic in this postmodern era, it does provide a careful analysis of social dynamics as an environment for the church. This classic offers at the very least a way of thinking theologically and ethically about our mission in a society now organized around consequences rather than systematic beliefs. In contemporary parlance, this means society is the "client" on which organized religion must do spiritual-mental therapy.

The synthesis of ethics that follows is not intended to be exhaustive. It is meant as a demonstration of how the type of ethics we believe affects our morality. For students of formal ethics, this synthesis may be a welcome opportunity to apply the insights of academic forebears to our contemporary ethical confusion, most particularly the clergy sex scandals.

I offer an instructive synthesis of clinical, theological, and sociological morality and ethics that has been developed in democratic capitalism. This is indeed a major dynamic of the social and individualistic thinking that makes sexual libertarianism a common assumption, even among those who profess the absolutist ethics of a Judeo-Christian heritage. In a sense then, our contemporary floundering is a predictable outcome of the confusion that has resulted because the "American Experiment" has had to blend absolute beliefs with our proclamation of liberty and free will. Trying to mix these is like trying to combine water and gasoline. So each of us now lives with some confusion about what is right and wrong. Many who have sincere religious beliefs find that the beliefs they claim as the center of their lives do not always guide their decisions and behavior. Under everyday pressures we often choose what is expedient or offers the least threat to our comfort over what we believe is right.

A well-known youth evangelist, speaking at a large gathering of Christian youth that I attended, asked the crowd to raise their hands if they believed it was wrong to lie. Almost all raised their hands. Then he asked how many of them would lie to get out of a bad situation. Again almost all raised their hands. When he asked how many saw a problem with their responses to these two questions, only a handful raised their hands. Older believers in my seminars and counseling appointments tell how they often feel guilty or confused when they realize their behavior does not match what they say they believe. What is the difference between these age groups?

A typical resolution to moral dilemmas is to compartmentalize—to proclaim our belief in an absolute theological ethics while living according to a secular ethics of consequences. This is fertile ground not only for compartmentalization but also for denial and hypocrisy—in individuals and in faith communities.

Another typical way to resolve moral dilemmas is to rationalize behavior that does not conform to our stated beliefs. In rationalizing we may make excuses, plead ignorance, blame someone or something for our moral failure, or say we will do better next time.

Our frequent moral dilemmas, confusion, and violation of our beliefs are a rather clear indication that our world is passing from the era when traditional beliefs typically guided our decisions and determined our behavior. Those beliefs still guide some of our behavior, but when we are honest with ourselves we can see that often we make our decisions by comparing likely consequences of optional behaviors. This means we entertain another set of beliefs for some decisions.

In the following analysis of contemporary ethics, the term *absolutist ethics* will be used to express the conflation of ethical systems based upon absolutes. The term *consequential ethics* will be used to express the conflation of pragmatic ethical systems.

The Premises of Absolutist Ethics

1. Truth is absolute. Here begins the ancient debate over whether or not truth as we observe it can be absolute, and if so, how this is determined. Absolutist ethics typically includes a priori and a posteriori assertions regarding what is absolutely true in our perceived reality. The assertion regarding truth is then grounded in revelations from God or posited as a universal experience in the human mind. Though there are variations in what is seen as absolute truth, the identifying factor in absolutist ethical systems is that whatever is regarded as truth is absolute. All following premises are based upon this assertion.

2. Truth can be known. Now comes the necessary connection between a transcendent reality and human perception. An absolutist ethics is obligated to connect the divine and the human. This connection is asserted primarily as a function of revelation from the divine to the human. The revelation can be imposed, as with creation. It can be proffered in a divine personality or in a spiritually discerning human interpreter. With this assertion of revelation comes a specific identity of God as its source. Further, God must be known through recognizable characteristics such as omnipotence, omniscience, and omnipresence that make a proclamation of the asserted, absolute truth believable. And further yet comes the mediation of this truth through a community of faith vowed to translate and demonstrate this truth in their lives.

3. One belief system is universally applicable. Because this identified truth is seen to be absolute, absolutist ethics must make the case that it is globally prescriptive. This is accomplished with further interpretation of the asserted absolute truth. For with an identifiable God, believed to have created all that is, it is no stretch to presume that God's revelation of truth must be proclaimed for all to hear and accept. Who better to do this than true believers, secular or religious?

In contrast, among more secular philosophical ethicists, Immanuel Kant (*Critique of Practical Reason* [1788]) offered an ethics he claimed could be globally prescriptive, simply because its goal is to benefit all persons. His categorical imperative urged people to always behave in ways that could become a universal standard. His system, though no longer prominent, became a valued model for ethicists who wanted to base ethics upon highest human concepts rather than upon a revelation from God.

4. Behavior that violates truth is unethical. When absolute truth is identified and codified, the code becomes the standard for all doctrine. Since there are various interpretations of the truth, however, deciding which behaviors are ethical and which are not becomes problematical. A consensus begins to emerge among these interpretations when certain controversial behaviors are practiced so commonly that they cannot be condemned easily or punished effectively (for example, living together without legal marriage, cutting corners on income taxes, watching X-rated movies, gender discrimination). Thus, absolutist ethics contains the seeds of its own evolution toward an ethics of consequences, even though it still prefers to control public ethics by controlling beliefs.

5. **Ethical behavior benefits all.** Life without ethics is unthinkable. But what kind of ethics is most effective in guiding life toward our Creator's purposes? At its best an absolutist ethics looks for caring and altruistic behavior as its ideals. Yet in a world of diversity it is compelled often to defend its views and try to enforce them when it has the power to do so. But then when there is enough diversity of beliefs in a given setting, absolutist ethics must choose between options. It must separate itself from those who will not conform to their beliefs and practices, or it can adapt its beliefs to practices that emerge in a consensus among diversities. This evolution again suggests that absolutist ethics has difficulty enduring as global interaction and interdependency continue to develop. As any ethics of absolute beliefs becomes less convincing and universal, its power to guide and control thinking and behavior lessens. So those who violate the mandated ethical boundaries begin to have less fear of condemnation and punishment, and less loyalty to this cause.

The Premises
of Consequential Ethics

For centuries, formal, absolute belief systems dominated intellectual and social settings, with a kind of erratic pragmatism operative on the streets, in the workplace, and in homes. People did their best to learn the ideals and yet did what had to be done in everyday life. In our postmodern (some add, post-Christian) world, diversity, change, and interdependent cultures make it more difficult to contrive or discern universal spiritual values applicable to all. Thus, the parallel constructionist movements called pragmatism, utilitarianism, relativism, and contextualism seem to offer a viable way to find workable guidance for behavior. We simply do what seems like a good idea at the time, then live with the consequences. Slowly we learn that all good (and bad) ideas have a long history, even if we just thought them for the first time.

Here is how consequential ethics looks when spelled out.

1. There are no absolutes, only consequences. This impatient presumption evolves from frustration, boredom, oppression, and a loss of trust in authority figures, perhaps even in God. Nothing seems dependable except what can be seen and demonstrated. Ideals and traditions still have value, but mostly as cautionary memories. The real reference points now are the consequences of human behavior, interacting pragmatically with the natural consequences of our planet and universe.

2. All behavior has shared, cumulative consequences. The notion of consequences that now guides much of human life is inadequate without memory. It also needs the wisdom derived from pain and failure and from pleasure and success. Consequences are relatively predictable, though interpretations vary. They may fade in influence, but their immediate use comes through incorporating them into decision making.

3. The self and environment are the reference points. Since an individual can't know for sure what others feel or need, the default position is to trust personal experience. An illusion develops that others feel and think as I do. Thus, we need an additional and more objective reference point, such as the environment. A sense of self-interest, coupled with feedback from the world around me, offers a reality check. And we can learn that it is in our best interests to act altruistically. G. E. Moore argued in

Principia Ethica (1903) that it is a matter of self-interest to seek the most good for the most people. Further, our environment, including this planet, becomes a mirror reflecting the value of our behavior. This is a significant shift in ethics, not because individualism hasn't existed before, but because so much freedom in behavior has not existed before in human history. With this much freedom, bad behavior is more likely.

4. **Decision making is the ultimate human behavior.** Since we make hundreds of conscious and unconscious decisions everyday, it is easy to underestimate the power of decision making. Human history has been dominated by hierarchies of controlling leaders who allowed freedom to decide only within the limitations of decisions they had already made. Multiple resources and empowerments are allowing ordinary persons to make immediate and lifelong decisions, based partly upon personal beliefs, but mostly upon choices of perceived consequences. This is another of our evolving paradigm shifts.

5. **Negotiation is the primary skill.** Wars, oppressions, and intimidation are necessarily yielding slowly to the skills of negotiation and mediation. The interactive and interdependent global family is running out of the space and victims needed to sustain violence and vengeance. Such haunting monsters of evil are everpresent. Yet their power to control by brutalization diminishes as democratically empowered human beings learn the full meaning of consequences and see the values in negotiating cooperation and peace.

6. **Fairness is morality.** The ordinary word "fairness" is becoming the premier concept of morality and ethics. It is even replacing archaic, legal definitions of justice. Anthropologists, missionaries, and business developers seem to agree that there is a nearly universal sense of fairness in the global family. Multiple examples of sharing, respectfulness, apology and forgiveness, and negotiation and consensus indicate the existence of an enduring primal tendency within normal human beings that thrives where fairness is opera-

tive. There are cultural diversities in this concept and its application, to be sure. Yet it seems to be a valuable conflation of altruism, justice, empathy, and the learned wisdom of consequences.

One of the strongest reasons for discovering, eliminating, and preventing sexual offenses is fairness—in its highest, altruistic, and spiritual meanings.

7. **Learning is experiential.** It is apparent that human beings are not born with an understanding of consequences. We are born with a potential for such understanding. The experience of consequences is the most effective teacher of ethics. Though irrational and oppressive consequences can be imposed where power and control preside, it is these very consequences, along with positive alternatives, that move human beings toward the wisdom of consequences. We must be taught and then learn the ennobling power of respect, negotiation, and love.

8. **Research on consequences is the key to the future.** God's creation is a chaos rich with creative potentials. Morphosis and social development are natural in creation. But we need history, consequences, and computers to provide the exponential learning necessary for a healthy, creative, global family and thriving ecology. Chaos in popular usage means disarray, incoherence, and failure. In quantum science and spirituality chaos means the creative churning of God's life-force (energy)—both unpredictable and yet dependable. If we desire to synchronize with the awesome creativity of God's dynamic creation, we must study fractals, holography, and energy. (For more information on quantum sciences, consult Ó Murchú 1997.)

9. **We know God and each other best through consequences.** Theology, confessions, and doctrine have their place. But their importance is fading as diversity, individuality, and creativity push us into consequential ethics. Consequences include continuing revelation (a consequence of listening reverently), pain (pangs of violating health), and joy (celebration of health, intimacy, and creativity). But consequences are mostly about learned realities. We

are learning, from consequences, that we cannot live without a divine being. We are learning, through consequences, that we cannot live without each other. We are learning, in consequences, that we cannot be healthy in an unhealthy environment. In organized religion we are learning, through consequences, that sick sexuality generates sick spirituality—and vice versa. And we are learning that consequences have consequences. God is in there somewhere, bigger than life. We do not need to invent God. We can learn God through the consequences of meditation, healing, and joy.

10. **Beliefs and values emerge from consequences.** The circle of spirituality is not completed by doctrines and laws. Rather, the circle is fulfilled in spiral form, as consequences accumulate, evolve, and form patterns. Consequences are like fractals. They are small, generative elements of God's sexual (creative) universe. When examined freely, they teach the power of belief—believing what we experience as we open ourselves to God's continuing "chaotic" purposes.

The relativity factor can be used to reject consequential ethics out-of-hand. Yet, if we think carefully, we realize that much of our lives are already lived by choosing what we think will work best rather than by careful analysis of religious doctrines. Further, all through religious history the great documents, including the canon of the Bible and the doctrines and polities of the denominations, were decided by voting rather than by absolute, unanimous fiats. Yet relativity is worrisome when used by undisciplined, unhealthy persons.

Application

The application of insights derived in analyzing the unannounced premises of the ethics of consequences can be done with an example of how consequential ethics has altered a key aspect of America's social philosophy. This sea change in our American philosophy of life not only reflects the negative influence of consequential ethics, it also offers insight into how an honest, asexual, altruistic perspective on life can shift to a polar opposite perspective.

Note the following guileless original version and the insolent contemporary version that has begun to replace the original. Even with this simplistic comparison, the inroads of abuse, violence, and irresponsible expressions of sexuality are apparent. This is what needs to be recognized by organized religion as it tries to understand the prevalence of sexual offenses, from pulpit and pew. For abusive sexuality is no longer only a matter of mental disorders and professional boundary violations; it is becoming a normal part of America's lifestyles. Entitlement thinking is its driving force.

The Traditional American Philosophy of Life
I work hard.
I live right.
I accept my just rewards.
In emergencies I sacrifice my rights for the benefit of the group.

The Entitlement Philosophy of Life
I have a right to what I want.
If I don't get what I want, I can blame someone.
When I find out who is to blame, I can punish them.
In an emergency, the group must sacrifice for my comfort.

Now some focusing questions for will help us apply the changing American philosophy of life to clergy sex scandals.

1. What effects does the traditional American philosophy of life have on sexual morality today?
2. Is the entitlement philosophy of life really dangerous to healthy sexuality?
3. How does your lifestyle reflect aspects of both American perspectives?
4. Does your perspective on healthy sexuality reflect one or both?

Conscience:
A Unique Human Motivation

Conscience is a subject related to the issues discussed in this book. It is, however, such a nebulous and controversial entity that a full discussion related to the issue of sexuality and spirituality is beyond the scope of this book. The inclusion of this brief mention of conscience simply acknowledges its historic standing in traditional morality. Contemporary perspectives tend to place more emphasis on behavioral dynamics and consequences.

Conscience includes such historic issues as free will and moral law, along with newer theories of society and the global village. I follow the lead of many contemporary theologians and psychologists who either ignore the issue we call conscience or give it only passing mention. From theologians Thomas Aquinas, John Calvin, Karl Rahner, Paul Tillich, and James M. Gustafson to developmental psychologists Jean Piaget, Erik Erikson, Lawrence Kohlberg, and James W. Fowler, we have an argumentative mixture of agreement that the human conscience exists along with multiple and conflicting views of what it is, where it comes from, how it is formed and developed, and how it functions in everyday life. I view conscience as an inner voice, with divine references, malleable in childhood, then formed by mentors and personal experience by young adulthood. Conscience becomes a kind of default religious faith (like a default program in computers) that can be ignored, followed, or manipulated for personal or social reasons. Sigmund Freud saw it as a judgmental inner overseer. James M. Gustafson (1984) sees it as a kind of exercise in self-manipulation as moral choices are made (his discussion of human freedom is particularly valuable). Social and developmental psychologists tend to see it as a process of socialization that goes through stages of development corresponding to emerging mental skills. Therapists tend to see it as a conditioned and undependable perspective regarding self and relationships. Clergy tend to see it as a flawed but useful human faculty that must be noted, but that needs a spiritual transformation in order to be a dependable guide for moral behavior. Whatever the viewpoint, it is apparent that the human conscience is real; it acts as a kind of personal compass or legal court system, and yet it must be guided by more precise and reliable public mores.

It has been hoped for centuries that human conscience would function as a kind of dependable common sense regarding the management of behavior and relationships. This can become reality in closely related groupings, such as family, neighborhood, or community of faith. In society, however, we are left with a general population wise enough to not violate common mores most of the time, and a legal system intended to control persons unwilling or unable to abide by moral consensus.

The term conscience is not used elsewhere in this book because of its unreliability. Yet a kind of inner voice is assumed for all human beings. With sexual misconduct, it is assumed that the inner voice is muted, flawed, or ignored. Human motivations, as in the agendas for human behavior presented in this chapter, are presumed to be guided by a combination of innate drives and social considerations that need continual attention in order to function healthfully and altruistically. I also assume here, as explained in the discussion of an ethics of consequences, that most of us now use both our default religious faith and an awareness of actual or expected consequences for behavior to guide our lives. It is apparent to those of us with lively faith in God's grace and the discernment provided by the Holy Spirit that human beings need more than their own ideas in order to live as our Creator intended us to live. A prime reason this book, and many others, is to offer a review of healthy religious faith and guidelines for living this faith in a chaotic and sexual world.

For a helpful summary of the contemporary understanding of conscience, consult the *Dictionary of Pastoral Care and Counseling* (Hunter 1990).

Summary

In this chapter I shift our attention from sordid, insidious, or unusual sexual behaviors that are scandalizing American clergy to the logical question about such behavior: Why do people act as they do? As the first part of a response, three general factors are cited and examined. One is the schema "agendas for human behavior," which summarizes psychological perspective on the three primary motivations for human behavior. This schema shows lifelong unconscious motivations that influence our sexual behavior.

The second is an ethical factor that provides a brief overview of two conflicting ethical perspectives that have a long history. The designations for these two perspectives are absolutist ethics and consequential ethics. These conflicting perspectives offer dissimilar guidelines for managing human sexuality and therefore introduce confusion rather than clarity. But they can be combined positively.

The third is a rudimentary version of America's evolving philosophy of life, from an integrity-altruism version to a more recent version that emphasizes individualism and entitlement. Even in this simplistic review the sea changes in America's philosophy of life can be noted. A new understanding of spirituality emerges as religious beliefs and consequences of behavior are combined.

Focusing questions are offered following each of the three influences on human behavior—psychological, ethical, and social. For, although there are no direct causes for sexual misconduct in any of them, the influence of each indicates a lessening of support for integrity, mental-spiritual health, and appropriate professional boundaries.

9.
HEALTHY SEXUALITY:
ITS JOYS, VARIETIES, AND AGENDAS

Sex: Adventure and Gift

SEX IS AN ADVENTURE OF BODY-MIND-SPIRIT. It offers the thrills of passion and orgasms and the disappointments of sexual dysfunctions and guilt trips.

Sex offers the deep joys of sexual intimacies, when bodies, minds, and spirits unite in fulfilled love. And it offers the sadness of broken relationships and shattered dreams.

Sex offers the choices of starting a new family by impregnation, then the pain and risks of pregnancy and the incredible joys of birth. Sex offers the troubling yet stimulating experiences of children growing up and discovering their bodies, and of parents establishing a healthy intimacy with them so they can understand God's gift of sexuality. Sex sometimes brings the experience of watching one child grow up fitting sexuality into a healthy lifestyle, while the other child never gets it right.

Sex offers us pastoral complexities of dealing with weddings where the partners have had many sexual encounters, with one other and sometime many others. It offers us the joy of officiating at baptisms when we know this child is growing up in a loving family. Sex offers us the privilege of sitting with a long-married couple as he tells her that he is gay. Then in the afternoon some time is spent in a young couple's home where the wife has asked that you come and offer prayers of thanksgiving as she tells her husband that after years of trying to become pregnant, it has happened. That evening you and your spouse are invited to dinner with your associate pastor who have one nearly perfect child and one who struggles with autism. Sunday morning, after the worship service, a young woman whispers in your ear that she needs to come talk with you about an abortion. You go home, have a nourishing lunch, and a nap. Then you and your spouse make love together. Is this what it's all about?

Sex cannot be a path of adventure if we have already denied its realities or turned it into a cul-de-sac. Yet, in order for it to be an adventure instead of a tragedy, we must have some kind of map and observe the speed limits. By now, those of us who are well along this path know that we need a combination of openness and wisdom in order to traverse this path safely. Carl R. Rogers, in *On Becoming a Person* (1961), taught that the first characteristic of a mature person is openness to experience. He had seen the human tendency to close off many opportunities in order to feel secure. God suggested openness to Jeremiah in a perilous and anxious time with an invitation to adventure, "Call to me and I will answer you, and will tell you great and hidden things that you have not known" (Jer. 33:3). We aren't prepared to hear "great and hidden things" from God if we think we already know it all.

This new millennium, for all its dangers and problems, can highlight the change and growth that is the message of transformation so clear in the Bible and religious history. Our ancient practice of trying to control God's energy and sexuality by codifying and mandating moral behavior doesn't fit when God's Holy Spirit is on the move. Leonard Sweet (1999) urges spiritual leaders to learn to swim in the new context of change. Swimming may be a useful first step in following God's leadership today. But the scope of transformations and speed of changes now require us to break out beyond material limits and learn to fly. *Plus Ultra!* [More beyond!] Only God can guide us out here.

Why make sex such a central issue in life and ministry? Because it already is. We are learning that when we get sex right, we are more likely to get life right. God has built creation around generativity—sexuality. Therefore sexuality and spirituality are inextricably intertwined. When we have a spiritual challenge, it is also a sexual challenge. When we have a sexual dilemma, it is also a spiritual dilemma. Carl Jung, the famous colleague of Sigmund Freud, said that in his experience every sexual problem is a spiritual problem, and every spiritual problem is a sexual problem.

To put it another way, as James B. Nelson (1986) does, we are "between two gardens." In one garden humankind is blessed, told to "be fruitful and multiply," and given dominion over all of creation. In the other garden humankind is provided with luxurious bliss but warned of eating from the tree of good and evil. This second garden has become the accepted metaphor for human morality and downfall. Organized religion must decide which garden is the real one. Do we begin our theology of sexuality with a blessing or a curse? For, although the second creation story portrays the disobedience of Adam and Eve as the cursed behavior, it was gender and sexuality that took the blame. If we accept the second story as our reality, then any salvation must include the redemption of gender and sexuality. Matthew Fox (1983 and 1999) has offered an experiential theology that posits the first garden as the key metaphor. His books teach the meaning of God's blessing through sexuality and help point the way to experiencing the blessing in our bodies. It seems that both metaphors are useful.

One spring a combination of events converged to generate a moment of illumination for me. I had been reading Joan Timmerman's *The Mardi Gras Syndrome* (1984) and rereading Nelson's *Embodiment* (1978). Professor Nelson has been a mentor to me for years, and Joan Timmerman is a friend whose prophetic insights into the relationship of sexuality and spirituality have helped focus my perspective.

During the afternoon free time at a training retreat I was leading for a denominational executive, I was sitting alone among the trees at the edge of the woods surrounding the retreat center. Our task was the construction of a code of ethics for clergy in that judicatory. As I sat quietly, a red fox suddenly emerged from the woods chasing a rabbit. She caught it, and after making sure it was dead, she carried it in her mouth back into the woods. Since it was spring, I assumed she was nourishing her kits or teaching them how to hunt. In my mind I explored the awareness that the fox's sexual adventures had produced those kits, and now she was obligated to care for them. Why did nourishing her offspring require killing an innocent rabbit? For some reason this episode connected with the purpose of our retreat. And I had to review the vagaries of sexuality that required terror and death for the rabbit in order to nourish the offspring of a sexual encounter. I had been teaching that sexuality was a gift from God, and that it was a basic dynamic in all of creation. Why did God create a planet where sexuality includes risk? How is risk a part of healthy sexuality?

As part of this illuminating experience, I then had a flashback to counseling appointments I had had recently. One was with a pastor's spouse who set an appointment to talk of how she could get her husband into marital counseling to work on their sexual problems. Another appointment was the anguished experience of helping a pastor tell his wife that he was gay. Yet another was a long phone conversation with a lay leader in a congregation who was worried their pastor was involved in sexual misconduct. I had also heard a rumor that the psychiatrist I used for medical referrals was going to be charged with sexual misconduct. It was reassuring to remind myself that many of my counseling cases were with persons who were managing their sexuality reasonably well. It was also reassuring to work with sincere denominational leaders at this retreat as they searched for ways to address clergy sexual misconduct and care for victims.

Sex has become organized religion's basic flaw. If we take time to discern sexual spirituality we can see its power to create or destroy, to bless or curse. Sex is a word that is now encumbered with many harsh realities and titillating fantasies. Organized religion, and each of us personally, are struggling to blend our management of sex with spiritual sexuality. This is a critical task, for it involves theology, public policy, and the stewardship of this planet.

Sexuality is a gift from our Creator that keeps on giving and giving and giving, whether we want more or whether we manage it for good or evil. Sexuality's function and objective are to generate, to create, to bring wholeness, and to bring pleasure. It is not a problem to be fixed. Organized religion needs to be fixed.

Being fixed does not mean patching the holes. Jesus reminded us of the folly in sewing a piece of material from a new garment on an old one (Luke 5:36). We can't fix sex, but we can open it to transformation. In order to understand spiritual transformation we must see it is different from denial, rationalization, and tinkering. Instead of making more rules to fix or control sex, our healing and transformation will come as we let sexuality be what it is.

God's gift of sexuality is a spiritual gift. It comes from God and therefore is sacred. It can bless our bodies, our minds, and our spirits, together. Sexuality is created into us as a primary dynamic of our spirituality. "Sex" is our abbreviation for sexual spirituality. It is what we do with our sexuality.

Sex can be healthy or unhealthy. Since its beginnings, organized religion has had the key to healthy sexuality. The key is love. Somehow, we already know this. Church and synagogue do rather well with love. We use the word a lot. We try to explain it. Yet we do not do well in connecting it with our personal versions of sex. Spiritual sexuality doesn't exist without love. Unhealthy sex does. Can human beings ever get it right—healthy sexuality? Yes, many do. Many more think they do.

Our mission, if we accept it, is to get deeply in touch with our sexuality, for it is at the core of our creativity and spirituality. And as we risk opening ourselves and our theology to spiritual sexuality, its transforming agent can fulfill a dynamic purpose, transformation.

Transformation has become a popular term in religion, for we all know it is basic to good religion. By making this word common, however, we endanger our understanding of it. Transformation has many synonyms: convert, metamorphose, transfigure, enlighten, and such. None of them means "to fix." They all indicate a radical, primary change. We have spiritualized the word transformation by trying to make it a mystical, theological ideal. Since spirituality is compartmentalized for many of us, we can then imagine, even pretend, transformation, and thus get virtual transformation. Transformation in its real meaning is more like metamorphosis—like watching a caterpillar become a butterfly. Transformation is already built into the caterpillar, as it is in us. The transforming agent for us is love. God is both creator and mediator of love ("God is love," 1 John 4:8). In our search for this beautiful dynamic, we have often mysticized it or tried to find it in sex.

There is a hopeful prospect in our present dilemma with sex. We can either try to fix it or allow love to transform it. The hope lies in seeking forgiveness, then opening ourselves to both the disciplines and the joys of true love. We already know how: Jesus (John 15:12) and Moses (Deut. 6:4) showed us. It's the doing . . . the living. . . . Sex alone will not suffice to fulfill our sexuality.

This book cannot produce this transformation nor even explain it completely. It offers some of the basic ingredients and stories, with a prayer shared by many that God will help us open ourselves to the sexual power of love.

For some years there has been an informal trend in religion to "do theology." Sexuality offers a valuable opportunity for this, because most of our theologies do not yet deal with sexuality in ways that are useful for the contemporary scene. Anyone who takes religious beliefs seriously is already rationalizing traditional teachings about sex. For though some of them are valuable, most are conceived and worded in ways that provide diminishing guidance for our lifestyles. We can do better than this.

One way is to spell out some simple definitions and theological premises and see how they fit God's purposes and our present experiences. The following are intentionally simplistic, in order to invite interaction and prayerful reassessment of what we say we believe.

Generic Definitions (with Many Variations)

The following definitions, theological postulates, and premises of sexuality are offered as informed and experiential perspectives rather than exhaustive absolutes. They are brief ways of organizing thinking about the complex issues of human sexuality. Variations are assumed. Interaction is encouraged.

1. Love. Love is beyond definitive description because its source is God, and because each person's need for love is unique. In human experience love is two-dimensional: attraction and intention. Attraction is the biochemical and social affinity between two persons, while intention is the pursuit of close relationship with the intent of mutual enrichment. Theologically (Christian), a tradition of three types of love accounts for variation: *philia* (Greek) = friendship; *eros* (Greek) = sexual attraction; *agape* (Greek) = sacrificial, unconditional caring. In popular usage, love can mean kindness, liking, preference, passion, and euphoria. In its moral/ethical ideal, love includes respect, reverence, altruism, and disciplined passion. Yet in real life love is chaotic—sometimes hot, sometimes cool, sometimes contented, sometimes conflicted, sometimes confident, and sometimes unsure. Love in the Bible is clearly about relationships and connectedness. The ideal is 1 Corinthians 13, which is read so sincerely at weddings. For many couples and families, it is a work in progress.

One of my favorite metaphors for love is "investment." Love as an investment is based on Matthew 6:21: "Where your treasure is, there will your heart be also." It doesn't cover all the bases, but thinking of a committed loving relationship as a bank account, an investment property, or even the stock market highlights a key dynamic of any good relationship, especially a committed love relationship. The laws of investment are simple: keep putting money in a reliable account or property; watch it carefully; do everything you can to enhance this investment; if it ceases to be a wise investment, withdraw.

Love is not like money, but it grows by investment. In a marriage, for example, paying caring attention to your partner, giving compliments, sharing in primary tasks, and developing a good sex and recreational lifestyle are investments that will keep your attention on the loved one and keep that person feeling loved. A prime requirement in investment is that it must be two-way. If your investment is not returning a fair profit, it makes little sense to continue investing in it. In a committed relationship, however, your may keep investing even though the benefits and effort are unequal. But in order for it to remain a healthy love, there must be an adequate return.

Is lust a part of love? Yes, because lust is the testosterone-estrogen biochemistry so natural in primates. It exists in its own right, whether as a part of love, or play, or abuse. Lust is not love, but it can enhance intimate love (more on intimacy later). The word lust has aversive associations, but it is common enough to be understood as a driving sexual passion. Libido is a related term popularized in Freudian literature but commonly misunderstood. We need a more acceptable word for the passionate dynamic in love. Passion is an acceptable word for me but not for everyone.

In recent years a new word for feelings of romantic attraction has come from scientific sexology. The word is *limerance* and means a blissful feeling associated with a particular person. Science can now identify biochemical factors and traceable pathways in the brain that characterize limerance. This offers research possibilities for understanding the causes, functions, and duration of romantic attraction, whether appropriate or inappropriate (limerance is discussed in Money 1999).

Love has other meanings, of course. What other healthy and unhealthy meanings does it have? How do you preach on love? How can love be translated into sexual behavior? James B. Nelson (1992) says "Our bodyselves are intended to express the language of love. Our sexuality is God's way of calling us into communion with others through our need to reach out, to touch, to embrace—emotionally, intellectually, and physically"(36).

2. Sexuality. Sexuality is a gift from our Creator. Generically, sexuality refers to the duality of gender required for reproduction and generativeness. Sexuality is also a function of spirituality. Since spirituality is the energy of God, since God is generative (witness continuing creation) and relational (witness the trinity or "us" of Gen. 1:26), we may understand God as sexual (generative) in presence and action (relational). How is gender related to sexuality? If sexuality is spiritual by definition, how does rape fit into it?

3. Sex. This is the human expression of sexuality—individual, relational, and interactive. Sex is a function of libido, sensual cues, and habit. It wants a close, passionate relationship, but it tends to focus on that which offers sensual or orgasmic pleasure. Sex is difficult—good sex, that is. Bad sex is easy, like jumping off a cliff. An intimate relationship is its highest expression (more later).

What don't you understand about sex (seriously)? How are you going to find out?

This may be a good time to reflect not only on these definitions but also on how they have been, and are, experienced in your life.

Theological Premises

The following theological formulations are not a new theology, but they constitute a fresh perspective on the relationship of sexuality and spirituality. We bring a lot of baggage to our theological and everyday thinking about sexuality. Albert Einstein said that we cannot solve today's problems with yesterday's thinking. Spiritually, this means we will need to be in an open and prayerful frame of mind (discernment) as we think about sexuality theologically. Discernment is a frame of mind in which we are prepared to follow the lead of God's Holy Spirit. These theological premises are a reverent effort to state the ineffable and to apply them to our lives with discernment.

1. God is love.
Love is focused spiritual energy.
Therefore, Love expresses God's creative intentions.

Application: God is the greatest being humankind can think of, according to St. Anselm. Then if God is love, according to 1 John 4:16, love is the greatest emotion.

Love, by definition, must be interactional. Therefore, God's love is intentionally relational.

2. The source of spiritual energy is God.
Spiritual energy is procreative.
Therefore, God is sexual.

Application: God is God, not a super human being. The Great "I Am" is spirit. We worship God "in spirit and truth." Our worship is a thankful, energetic response to God's creative presence and to God's material (crystallized energy), creative (sexual) universe. Chaos is the new insight into God's creative energy, now being

explored by the quantum sciences and prophetic spiritual leaders.
The Chaos concept is not about disruption, disorder, and lawless-
ness but about the massive, churning rhythms of spiritual energy
out of which God created a dynamic material world. Genesis 1 is
the best effort by ancient writers to put these awesome, ineffable
realities into human concepts and words. This creative energy of
God continues to transform creation in timeless fashion as we live
our everyday lives. We are part of this drama. By God's mandate
and blessing we have responsibility to help manage this material
world with spiritual insights.

3. Sexuality is passionately generative.
Sexuality creates new life.
Therefore, sexuality is spiritual.

Application: New life, aging creatures, and recycling flora and
fauna are all part of the generative characteristics of God's spiritual
energies. Sexuality is a union of the creative forces that regenerate
existing life and create new life forms. Sex is our human procre-
ation efforts and the passionate experience of God's creative
energy. Human creativity, in its healthy forms, is our stewardship
of the earthly part of God's creation. Unhealthy creativity is our
sin. Sin is our violation of God's mandate for healthy creativity.

4. Humankind is created out of God's sexuality.
Humankind is sexual.
Therefore, people relate to God's creation sexually.

Application: Though we are each unique creatures, we are active
parts of the larger creation. When we try to disconnect or abuse
our connections, our relationships, we violate the synergy of God's
creation. Sexuality is relational, connectional, with all else that is
created as sexual. Disconnection and abuse are our sins.

5. Jesus modeled sexuality.
Jesus broke gender barriers.
Therefore, Jesus is sexual in new ways.

Application: For Christians, Jesus is the God-given model of human life in which sexual generativity is lived without emphasis on gender or sexual expression. We do not know about Jesus' unique and yet common experiences of human sexuality. He may have been celibate, gay, or divorced. Since he was male and sexual, what is recorded of his personal life may be understood as emphasizing what was most important about sexuality. The records of his life show that his generativity included caring love, judgment on sin and evil, justice, healing, the transformation of sinful lives, and celebration of healthy living. It is part of healthy sexuality to see these as standards. They do not deny or demean sexual intercourse, bearing children, or orgasmic pleasure; for these, when done healthfully, do not violate the sexual standards he demonstrated. (I feel no competence to express this aspect of sexuality for Jewish traditions.)

6. The Holy Spirit helps us discern God.
To "know" God is a high sexual experience.
Therefore, sexuality leads us beyond sex.

Application: Part of God's revelation to the prophet Isaiah was a reminder that "As the heavens are higher than the earth, so are my ways higher that your ways, and my thoughts higher than your thoughts" (Isa. 55:9). Yet God also spoke to and through the prophet Jeremiah in these words: "[In those days] I will put my law within them, and I will write it on their hearts" (Jer. 31:33). To have God working "within" us is surely a generative, sexual process, expressed in God's "higher" ways. This is a metaphor and reminder of the sacredness of sexuality, as well as the creative, redemptive, and joyful purposes of sex for us.

7. *The* Imago Dei *created in us is a stewardship of life.*
God creates and nurtures.
Therefore, stewardship is sexual.

Application: An ineffable God has expressed God-ness in creation, in each of us. We are the embodiment of that which is
greater than ourselves. This is our visible, experiential mode.
God's creative energy includes nurture of what is created. Our
mandate is the nurture/stewardship of a generative/sexual creation. Exploitation is a violation of this mandate and therefore is
our sin. Our faithful stewardship is expressed in love, sharing, reverence, justice-making, healing ministries, and celebrations of generative sexuality.

These syllogistic theological premises are much too simplistic
to exhaust the relationship between spirituality and sexuality. I
offer them as a catalyst for prayerful consideration. Their true
value will occur as we inventory and evaluate what we actually
believe about sexuality and the way we practice it.

Significant Issues of Sexuality

Gender Differences

Gender differences are the stuff of everyday humor. They are also
points of controversy now that women have more freedom to be
equal partners with men. No matter our prejudices and assumptions, common sense tells us that men and women vary in significant ways. We also recognize that differences and uniqueness add
spice to relationships as well as vulnerabilities.

Following is a short list of some scientific brain and behavioral
differences that emerge from recent research. These will not be
surprising to many, but they are interesting and significant.

1. Men tend to be more easily and frequently aroused sexually than women. How do we equalize this difference?

2. Women typically have more neural pathways connecting the right and left hemispheres of the brain through the corpus callosum than men. This means that women can use both cerebral hemispheres more readily than men. Men tend to use the left hemisphere (verbal and organizing skills) more consistently. Who makes the rules?

3. When angry, men tend to become louder and more aggressive, while women tend to become silent. Is one tendency better than the other?

4. Women tend to want a comfortable setting and loving preparations in order to enjoy sexual intercourse, while men want prompt gratification. Adjustments or failure to adjust to this difference usually is a significant factor in intimate relationships.

5. Both genders tend to have a hard time believing the actual differences that exist between them. Both may think they know their partner fully, or they make jokes and roll their eyes over this one. But women typically try harder to understand men than vice versa. Can a relationship be happy if the woman makes most of the preference adjustments?

According to Carl Jung, we human beings have both an *anima* (female archetype) and an *animus* (male archetype) in our unconscious mind. This theory suggests that each of us has varying attributes of both genders present in some form.

Although it is not a popular concept among inclusive language and unisex thinkers, there are some who cite evidence that women and men have different minds, designed and developed for different functions. For discussions of gender differences, see Moir and Jessel 1991, Money 1981, Howard 2000, Jung 1964, and Ridley 1993.

Sexual Pleasure in the Brain

Brain research has tended to focus on negative aspects of brain stimulation (pain, anger, fear, etc.) rather than pleasure. However, a recent essay by Kent C. Berridge entitled "Pleasures of the Brain" (2003) notes some such research findings. Several areas of the brain can be stimulated with electrodes to produce pleasurable sensations, some of which lead to powerful sexual excitation or responsiveness to sexual cues. Further, there are "hedonistic pathways" traceable in the brain, from the brain stem to the limbic system to the prefrontal cortex. Stimulation (electrodes or hormones) in the brain stem lead to instant responses. Stimulation in the limbic system adds emotion to the responses. When memory and conscious thought routes these stimuli on to the prefrontal cortex, judgment is added to the memories of past stimuli and responses.

Researchers note the need for more research on pleasurable and sexual stimulation of the brain. Yet, when this recent research is added to what is already known about the "pleasure centers" of the brain and about alcohol and drug reactions, it is apparent that some pleasurable experiences become very attractive because they excite areas of the brain where these sensations are interpreted as highly pleasurable. By implication, if a person experiences any cues or stimuli through these sensual pathways and does not consciously consult significant memories before acting, the responses can become compulsive and irresponsible.

Such brain research is a valuable reminder that our sexual behavior can become compulsive, addictive, and irresponsible if we do not learn how to manage pleasure and sexual stimuli wisely.

A Sex Epidemic

HIV/AIDS, abortion, contraception, sexually transmitted diseases—these and other sex-related issues continue to trouble organized religion, like a background roar to which we have become accustomed. It is beyond the purview of this book to cover all sex conflicts, but it is useful to consider one that is a worldwide epidemic with deadly consequences. HIV/AIDS is a haunting malady because it has mushroomed into a deadly reality in such a shockingly short time, It is haunting also because it reveals the staggering amount of what we call promiscuity around the world, including the abusive behavior of men who infect their spouses (and the consequences of parentless or infected children). Further, in the U.S. we have the attitudinal residue of many who blamed the AIDS epidemic on homosexual behavior. For many in organized religion, AIDS has awakened compassion for victims of their own sexual misconduct and for others who are victimized by this misconduct. There are not many survivors. The AIDS issue is not only about a tragic and dangerous worldwide epidemic, it is also about individuals who experience this devastation personally. Our compassion and resources must flow toward such human suffering, no matter our prejudices and confusion.

For those of us not personally touched by the experience of HIV/AIDS, this phenomenon is a wake-up call. The ungoverned passions, the victimized spouses, the parentless and infected children and families—all remind us that there are mixed and life-threatening factors in any undisciplined sex. Moreover, this epidemic is not just "out there" and among "those people"; it is in our midst. I hear of cases of AIDS among pastors and lay leaders more frequently now. And I recognize that the great outpouring of prayers and support for AIDS victims in organized religion is a living of our faith in difficult and controversial situations. Yet there are still many who close their hearts in prejudice. We can pray, however, that even those sitting in judgment or living in denial will hear the warning messages about the consequences of sexual misconduct.

Our young people seem to be getting the message, albeit slowly. Even though they resist listening to the warnings of adult authority figures, they too can read and hear about the negative consequences of sexual misconduct. In families, in congregations, and in schools we must help our inexperienced and passionate youth manage their vulnerabilities sensibly. Nearly every major religious publishing house now publishes curriculum to instruct us in applying our beliefs effectively to personal and group sexuality. Concern, compassion, prayers, and informed instruction are no longer optional for our youth.

Self-Sex as Common Sex

Taboos and restrictions have not ended nor controlled self-pleasuring and masturbation over the centuries. But they have left a heritage of shame, fear, and guilty confusion for those who need a sexual outlet that does not abuse others. Religious teachings about the misuse of semen and declarations that only husband-wife intercourse was allowable left many believers with a dilemma. Not only has there been a heritage of shame and fear, but the weight of responsibility for contraception and "keeping a husband happy" was on a woman's shoulders.

With the advent of Kinsey, Pomeroy, Masters and Johnson, Kaplan, Money, and others, scientific sexology began to quantify, even with questionable statistics, the sexual practices and consequences of American sex. Raising of public awareness of the realities of sexuality and sex through these resources has been liberating. Yet we now also have a general attitude among many young people that there are no truly dangerous consequences to having sex whenever there are opportunities. The tragic consequences of young lives burdened with scars and irresponsible pregnancies tempts many leaders and parents to try to advocate "total abstinence" and "Just say no." On the other hand, some parents and schools still try to avoid responsibility for mentoring youth during vulnerable years.

Self-sex, solo sex, self-love, and similar terms are being used now to avoid the aversion attached to the term masturbation. Better terminology helps, but it is consequences that change thinking and social policy—sometimes even theology. There is little credible evidence of harm with masturbation, except for possible heart attacks or boredom and loneliness. It is now common knowledge that most people masturbate at some times in their lives. More useful, however, is the widespread experience that masturbation can help avoid many social and marital problems, such as spousal abuse, AIDS, unwanted pregnancies, and some forms of sexual misconduct. But we also know that masturbation can become addictive and can distract from marital satisfactions. When we know both the negative and positive consequences, we have a responsibility to share this information with those who need it.

Noted sexologist Betty Dodson, in her book *Sex for One* (1996), writes, "Masturbation is a primary form of sexual expression. It's not just for kids or for those in-between lovers or for old people who end up alone. Masturbation is the ongoing love affair that each of us has with ourselves throughout our lifetime. In the age of AIDS you'd think we could at least celebrate masturbation as the safest sex" (3).

The idea of safe sex between two persons is an illusion, of course. For even with condoms, sexually transmitted diseases and unwanted pregnancies occur, besides the guilt trips and anxieties. Further, our dire warnings to youth and a requirement of total abstinence in order to gain our approval is unrealistic. Warnings do not stop the flow of testosterone and estrogen, nor curiosity and their need to feel love. Trying to stop sexual expression in young people is like damming a river. The water has to go somewhere. We can offer safer outlets. Self-sex is one.

Ironically, it is the pleasure of self-sex that frightens many who advocate for the exclusivity of marital sex. Youth and adults suspect the truth. Further, our denials and restrictions keep us from celebrating both sex and healthy sexuality in varied forms. After all, God created us with built-in sexuality. It can't be all bad.

Gay-Lesbian Sex

As is the case with other varieties of sexuality, homosexuality is now in public consciousness. This polarizes many groups and relationships. Growing awareness of its prevalence, and the negative and positive aspects of gay-lesbian lifestyles, will lead eventually to changes in attitudes and public policy. The same is true in organized religion. We can see how many taboos and prejudices have faded in recent years as knowledge and familiarity grew. Once men and women sat on opposite sides of sanctuaries. Once women could live together with public approval, while men could not. Once homosexual persons were stoned or lynched, with the approval of religious authorities. Before 1973 the American Psychiatric Association classified homosexuality as a sexual deviation. Now it presumes homosexuality to simply be a variation of human sexual response. Yet much of organized religion still holds to a condemnation of homosexuality with less biblical evidence than there is against divorce, and even though we know the church has ordained gay priests and pastors for centuries.

I have done psychotherapy with gay and lesbian pastors over the years and find myself understanding better that homosexuality is not a choice, it is a recognition. A gay-lesbian lifestyle versus a virtual heterosexual lifestyle is a choice. It is too strong an orientation in many children of God to be remanded into our frightened prejudices. I have had two counseling relationships where gay-lesbian pastors changed their orientation from homosexual to heterosexual. They came to me with a strong, healthy desire for this change on their parts. Both had effective support systems, and we planned for and completed long-term counseling. I have had many more who recognized their homosexual orientation and sought pastoral counseling to assist them in accepting this identity, and then growing into healthy expressions of it. Several of them indicated that they knew of gay clergy who abused other gay clergy.

In writing this book I have reviewed my case files and read recent literature on gay-lesbian sexuality. Two of the most outspoken and highly competent researchers and advocates that I have encountered are John Boswell, late Professor of History at Yale

University, who wrote the landmark book, *Christianity, Social Tolerance, and Homosexuality* (1980); and Carter Heyward, Professor of Theology at Episcopal Divinity School, Cambridge, Massachusetts, who has written extensively. Her moving personal story is exceptionally troubling (*Staying Power,* 1995).

It is my personal friendship and conversations with gay-lesbian pastors that informs my perspective most appreciatively. As I began writing this book I asked an excellent pastoral colleague if he would sit down with me and tell me about his life. He graciously agreed. I heard a story that sounded very comfortable, in spite of some family difficulties, encounters with homophobic prejudice, and professional concerns. When I asked him, as I have asked other interviewees, what his vision of a healthy sex life is, he responded by saying it is the same as for any of his gay-lesbian friends: to live in a committed sexual relationship, to have a comfortable home, to have healthy, happy friends, to pay bills and taxes, to raise healthy children, and to enjoy the blessings of pastoral ministry. That sounds healthy to me.

The Joy of Intimacy

I know of no greater joy than intimacy. This is not another name for sex or close friendship, although it includes these. It is the name for the best of all human relationships. Intimacy is no small achievement. It seems like it should be a natural outcome of love and marriage, but it isn't. My working definition of human intimacy is "consistent, two-way, emotional closeness by agreement." This is a functional definition, for it contains the necessary dynamics of intimacy. You may have a definition that works for you. I hope so, for intimacy is unique to each couple. Take a look at the five dynamics I have seen work for many couples, as well as in my marriage.

1. Consistency is important because human passions ebb and flow. Without intentional investments in the relationship, on a regular basis, we are limited to mercurial episodes of intimacy. In other words, we need to discipline ourselves to feed a relationship, even when we do not feel like it, for this nourishes the closeness we each need.

2. **Two-way relationship** is important, lest one partner become the giver and the other the taker. This is not the same as keeping score. It means partnering, sharing, and adapting. Dominance has little value in intimacy. Marriage stereotypes and gender limitations can be avoided if leadership roles are flexible, and each persons' needs are accommodated. This two-way dynamic is not easy to achieve, for each of us has some kind of model for it in our heads that may or may not fit a partner's or family member's model. Two-way communication is where two-way intimacy begins and is nurtured.

3. **Emotions** are significant because they are the primary ingredients of our experience. Emotional bonding between persons is the core of intimacy. This is one of the reasons males in our culture typically have more difficulty with intimacy than females. Men have been programmed to deemphasize emotions and feelings, emphasize rationality, and forgo bonding and settle for encounters. Emotions are the engines that drive personal lives and relationships. Feelings are the conscious reactions that can trigger emotions, or the reactions to an emotion itself. Feelings are more fragile, fleeting, and erratic, while emotions are deeper, more reflective, and more enduring. Talking about them openly and managing them together keeps them from sabotaging intimacy. Love is the key emotion. But it is not automatic, it is a learned emotion, and it is based upon listening, caring, and sharing.

4. **Closeness** is the concept we most readily attach to intimacy. Yet the desire and need for closeness ebbs and flows. Sometimes one or both partners needs alone time in order to savor togetherness again. It can be difficult to be close. A cliché says that marriage is like two porcupines trying to make love. They first have to learn what to do with the quills. Closeness can be a fantasy unless

we learn how to make it attractive for both partners. Distance and private agendas starve intimacy. Closeness is necessary for intimacy. Being able to see, touch, talk about, and experience each other's presence is what intimacy is all about. This, of course, requires us to see and experience the other person as he or she really is—both defects and assets. Without this unconditional acceptance and appreciation, we are married to a fantasy rather than to a real person. We need to note here that in our erotically saturated society, closeness usually means sex, especially to men. In this definition, intimacy includes sex but is not limited to or defined by sexual intercourse.

5. Agreement is both an old and a new ingredient in intimacy. It has always been necessary to have agreements if two or more people are to live together in safety and comfort. But, in human history, such close relationships as marriage, family, and friendships were almost always based upon gender and social roles. Women performed one set of roles and men another. The goal was to do one's part as well as possible and to cooperate.

In recent years we have applied the ideal of equality to intimacy. We believe we can conceptualize it, but producing it together in the relationship on which we depend for affection and support requires intentional, shared effort. Negotiation is a necessary skill. None of us can impose our personal definition of equality on another person—not if we want intimacy. Negotiation—and most other interactions in intimacy—works best when it takes place in a context of the "magic" words: "Please," Thank you," and "I'm sorry." In fact, these expressions constitute an "attitude," a version of love, and are worthy of discussion. Families, teams, and congregations function much better when these words are understood and used regularly.

Marriage is not the same as intimacy. But it can be. An intimate marriage is one of the greatest deterrents to sexual misconduct and one of the deepest joys of living.

The Sexuality of Our Planet

We all learn about "the birds and the bees," but we may never have learned that the creative functioning of our planet is based upon sexuality. In the Bible and in traditional theology we learn about original creation and about human sexuality, but not the realization that our planet functions in sexuality. There are necessary forces such as gravity, light, atmosphere, and precipitation. But these do not produce life. Seeds, pollination, and copulation generate life. And it is the nurturing dynamic of sexuality that makes life thrive.

As we pay more attention to the health of our planet, we will see its sexuality more clearly. In this book we are noting that sexuality and spirituality go together, for our Creator is sexual and has built this dynamic into all of creation. The sexuality of God's creation is a hidden ingredient in biblical literature. It will be important to discover it if organized religion is to take its rightful place in the stewardship of this sexual planet.

Ken Wilbur, the noted philosopher of ecology, has provided a massive scholarly book, *Sex, Ecology, Spirituality: The Spirit of Evolution* (2000), that describes his version of the sexuality and spirituality of this planet. It is a rich resource from outside of traditional religion. Other scientists are beginning to combine their scientific insights with spirituality. From inside religion, John Polkinghorne, Professor of Mathematical Physics at Cambridge and an Anglican priest, wrote *Quarks, Chaos and Christianity* (1996); Diarmuid Ó Murchú, a priest and social psychologist in London has given us *Quantum Theology* (1997). And from inside the field of pastoral counseling Howard Clinebell has given us *Ecotherapy: Healing Ourselves, Healing the Earth* (1996).

It is encouraging to note that conceptions of a spiritual planet with sexual generativity are coming from quantum sciences, medicine, philosophy, psychology, and religion. Our old ideas of spirituality and sexuality are showing their age. These are times when the

world and religion break out of their traditions and follow the God
who said to Isaiah, "I am about to do a new thing" (Isa. 43:19).

Summary

In this chapter I explore the idea that sex is an adventure. A review
of how often sexual issues occur in congregations reminds us that,
although we are reluctant to speak openly of sex and sexuality in
organized religion, it is continually occurring in some form.

In order to clarify significant issues of sexuality in religion,
generic definitions of love, sexuality and sex are offered, followed
by a formulation of a theological perspective that recognizes the
combination of sexuality and spirituality.

Finally, seven significant themes in sexuality are reviewed: gender differences, sexual pleasure in the brain, the sex epidemic, self-
sex, gay-lesbian sex, intimacy, and the sexuality of our planet.

10.
THE JOYS OF HEALTHY SEX

ORGANIZED RELIGION must also embrace its light side. In chapter 7 we faced the dark side. The light side includes human sexuality. And, if we understand this and practice it, the light side includes sex. (Remember that sexuality is God's gift of generativity and caring, and sex is our management of this gift.)

My favorite version of the Advent drama is the account in John 1 where Jesus is described as "the light" that comes into the world to teach us about "life" from God. When we accept this light, we are "enlightened" (John 1:4, 9). It seems easier to see the world, ourselves, and sexuality, however, from the dark side, for this is what our fear (the most powerful of all human emotions) pays attention to. To take our light side seriously requires a transformation—a conversion. We have to graduate out of fear and into love. Fear distorts love, but "perfect love casts out fear" (1 John 4:18). In chapter 9, I examined sex as an adventure. In this last chapter we may savor our light side, our healthy side. Our light side is more than sex, but it includes sex and sexuality. These are as powerful as fear; in fact are more powerful, unless repressed. We need boundaries for both love and fear.

Sex is better when we are healthy. So is almost everything else. Sex is best when it is enfolded in love.

We all know this, but somehow this knowledge doesn't cause us to change our unhealthy thinking and lifestyles—until we get sick or become impaired. Then we assume we can pay someone to make us well, or take some pills to override the consequences of poor health habits.

The dilemma for most Americans is that we believe we are "normal." For normal means the way we usually feel and live, and we have a right to live this way. But according to former U.S. Surgeon General David Satcher, our normalcy is a kind of pre-sickness. American normal is setting many of us up for serious illness or impairment. According to Dr. Satcher, 55 percent of Americans are overweight, and 62 percent exercise too little to sustain good health. Further, the United States leads all industrialized nations in the top five serious diseases, except for HIV/AIDS. In 2001 we spent one and a half trillion dollars on health care, and the cost is rising. These statistics do not include the incidence and costs of mental and spiritual illnesses. It is clear that having the most advanced medical facilities in the world does not save us from ourselves.

Clergy in previous generations often led the nation in health statistics. Not anymore. Ministers Life & Casualty Company insured life and health for only clergy for many years, and it made a fine profit. But several years ago it had to merge with another insurance company and began to insure the general public in order to stay profitable.

Why make a point of this, when pastors somehow manage to get into the pulpit each Sunday? Because the clergy role can so easily conceal our unhealthiness from the congregation and from ourselves. My research and experience with pastors across the United States indicate that our profession is experiencing four persistent maladies that are easily camouflaged by the way we manage our pastoral role. Depression, burnout, role confusion, and sexual misconduct are "normal" for a significant number of pastors (see chapter two for a fuller discussion). Of course, this is occurring in other helping professions as well. The point, however, is that we, more than others, have adequate resources to stay healthy in body-mind-spirit, and we have a calling to do so. Yet our depression can look like pastoral conscientiousness, our burnout like normal pastoral busyness, our role confusion like changing with the times, and our sexual misconduct like pastoral cordiality. "I didn't even know I was sick" is a common report when illness or impairment strikes. In our indulgent and privileged society it is easy to live "the good life" right up until the day of our heart attack, or until we are in bed with a parishioner.

A Good Pastor on the Edge

Cal Hopkins was doing fine. He was very busy, as successful or "effective" pastors are expected to be these days. His growing congregation of several hundred members was located in a small town near a major metropolitan area. The church building was historic and located on a well-known river. Many professionals and laborers who worked in the city but preferred small-town ambiance lived within driving distance of Cal's church. The congregation had developed an intense style, with many programs and small study-support groups. There were normal conflicts and antagonisms, yet the congregation absorbed these into its stimulating and creative attitude.

Cal was gregarious, competent, and active in all phases of the congregation's life, and that of the community. He traveled into the city often to make hospital calls and attend study events. He and his wife, Betty Ann, had three children in lower grade and middle schools. She was a professional financial advisor working part-time for a prominent investment firm.

I learned of Cal's secret life only after several informal lunches we shared. We met at a seminar I did for area clergy, and he asked if we could have lunch. At our first lunch it was apparent that he wanted to cite his successes. By the end of our conversation it was also apparent that beneath the jovial exterior, he was troubled. He asked to set another lunch date. I countered by suggesting that we make an appointment to meet at my pastoral counseling office. His reluctance led to another lunch meeting. This time his anxieties were apparent from the beginning. He apologized for his weight, ordering cocktails, the handful of pills he took after lunch, and taking so much of my time. To postpone effusive revelations for a more appropriate setting, I asked some general questions and then referred to the seminar he had attended where I spoke of unfitness among pastors and some generic remedies. As we finished, I again suggested an appointment, but he insisted on meeting at this restaurant again. Realizing the importance of this process to him, I agreed. He always picked up the meal check.

At our next lunch he arrived early and arranged for us to sit in a secluded area of the restaurant. As soon as I sat down he poured out a story of growing awareness that, in spite of his professional achievements, his personal life was deteriorating in serious ways. He was overeating to compensate for anxious guilt feelings, drinking more alcohol to assuage his suspicions about rumors in the congregation, and becoming so busy with church work that he could no longer prepare adequately for his sermons and classes. When he was at home, he was spending more time watching TV and falling asleep in his recliner. The children were at home less, and Betty Ann was distancing herself from him. The secret part was his continuing indulgence in pornography, compulsive masturbation, and occasional visits to a sexual massage parlor. He had become infatuated with a woman in the congregation with whom he often worked on congregational projects. It was his fantasizing about her sexually to the point where he considered inviting her to travel to a church conference with him that finally forced him to break through his denials of how unfit he had become. For he realized that such an assignation would likely result in disaster.

After listening to his anguished confession, I acknowledged his pain and the dangers in his lifestyle. And he acknowledged the reality I shared with him, that a thorough transformation of his lifestyle was needed. Now he was ready to visit me in the office. It was reassuring, in our office appointments, to see his ego strength, his healthy fear of what was happening, and his ready acceptance of the prescriptions we developed for physical-mental-spiritual recovery and fitness. One of the prescriptions was for his marriage and family and required the involvement of Betty Ann and their children.

Cal had caught himself before most of the disastrous consequences of his overeating, drinking, and escapism caught up with him. He has since chosen health and fitness instead of self-destruction and boundary violations. Over a period of several months Betty Ann and the children helped in developing a healthy family lifestyle.

The last I heard from him was in his Christmas letter. His hand-written note on the back indicated that he and the family are enjoying a life of disciplined and reassuring fitness.

I include this story in a chapter on health and fitness to help clarify some issues important in understanding the relationship of health to clergy boundary violations. Much of this book has been devoted to a discussion of the worst, the bad, and the questionable scenarios of clergy sexual misconduct that we read about in media coverage. But Jacob in the generic story of chapter 2, and now Cal's story reflect the reality that, while some pastors commit gross offenses, even more are sincere, competent pastors caught in boundary violations that do not make scandals. Such situations need to be noted and remedies sought. Pastors who slip across shadowy boundaries may not make headlines or devastated victims, but the damage is real. Pastors who allow themselves to become physically, mentally, and spiritually unfit are unable to fulfill their call to faithful pastoring to the best of their ability. They are compromised, distracted, and disconnected from the discernment and empowerment available to healthy pastors. Such a condition is a serious loss for the church. Further, such pastors are at grave risk for boundary violations. Jacob got caught in his own consequences, while Cal looked over the edge and pulled himself back just in time. These are more common experiences among clergy than we want to believe. Pastors who are keeping themselves healthy in body-mind-spirit are much less likely to commit boundary violations, and they are much more likely to experience the joys of pastoring.

You may find it helpful to take a few minutes, before Cal's story fades in your memory, to make a list of the boundaries he violated. As it happens, other boundaries are often violated before the sexual one is crossed. When we allow ourselves to be a "star," when we abandon our parental role in the family, when we try to carry the church on our backs, when we violate good nutrition boundaries, when we overindulge in psychotropic substances and such, we have crossed so many boundaries that it is easy to cross the one that may victimize others tragically—and make headline news.

Both of these pastors illustrate one of the fallacies of American health illusions, namely, believing a person can be healthy in only part of himself. In truth, when either body, or mind, or spirit is unhealthy, this makes the other two vulnerable also. And being healthy spiritually ("on fire for the Lord!" or "dedicated to caring for the homeless") does not guarantee that a pastor has a healthy mind and body. Sooner or later the unhealthy parts of personhood infect the others.

Our small, parochial ideas of sex, love, and health are no longer adequate. As noted earlier, it is easy to think of health as if it is what's normal. We can do better than that. We must do better than that if we are to live and serve as our Creator intended.

The emerging national crusade for health offers us a prime opportunity to help lead the way into total health, not just physical or mental health but into "well being," as Howard Clinebell (1992) terms it. Medicine is leading the way (Herbert Benson, Dale Matthews, Larry Dossey, Rudolph Ballentine, and others), and religion is catching up (Morton Kelsey, Abigail Rian Evans, Matthew Fox, Margaret Kornfeld, and others). Psychologists are adding it to their agenda (James Fowler, Robert Sardello, Rollo May, Judith Orloff, and others). Holistic health will not become wholistic health until spiritual health, mental health, and physical health are seen as inextricably intertwined.

It seems difficult for organized religion to accept a leadership role in the national crusade for health. Even though the church has been a leading source of healing and health in previous centuries, since the Renaissance it has relinquished this role to medicine. And with the advent of psychology, organized religion has left mental health to its practitioners. This means that after the body and mind are split off, whatever is left over must be the province of religion. The result is that "salvation" and "love," two of religion's favorite subjects, leave the body and mind on their own. We can do better than that.

We can see this division of labor in the popular definitions of health, as offered by these four disciplines, each of which assumes it can make human beings healthy:

- medical definition: the absence of illness and impairments
- psychological definition: the absence of mental illness and behavioral dysfunctions
- alternative medicine: all systems in harmony and balance
- religious definition: connection with God through healthy relationships.

Principles of Biblical Wholeness

We can define health in the spiritual sense through the use of the word "wholeness" (Hebrew: shalom). Check out these five principles of spiritual wholeness, derived from Holy Scripture and from the contemporary theologians emphasizing it.

1. Wholeness is unifying. It unites body-mind-spirit. It unites us with each other. It unites all of creation with God (John 1:3, 12, 13).

2. Wholeness is based on spiritual health. This means that spirituality is the context for health. This does not mean that wholeness is ethereal, incomprehensible, and illusory but that wholeness is not divisible, and it is our connection to all of creation. Medicine, psychology, and science are now recognizing this spiritual context. We must be prepared to help this new world understand that spirituality is not a set of doctrines. It is God's energy available to us all (John 4:24; Gal. 15:16-26).

3. Wholeness is corporate and inclusive. We can't be whole alone. The interaction and interdependence of the geofamily are reminders that we cannot control and hoard God and God's resources for ourselves. We believe God wants to move all of creation toward wholeness (Rom. 12:3-8; 1 Cor. 12; John 15:1-7).

4. Wholeness is not perfection. It is a process of healing and growth that includes the realities of human life. Wholeness includes our disorders, pain, and sins, not to indulge them but to provide healing and support that respects our individuality. We can participate in wholeness even on our bad days. For when we accept God's offer to participate in wholeness, we come as we are, but with grace-filled and shared possibilities (Phil. 2:12-13; 2 Cor. 12:6-10; Rom. 7:14—8:6).

5. Wholeness is transforming. It is dynamic in positive ways. It is God's "Chaos" in action (remember the quantum science's definition of Chaos discussed earlier). Wholeness is not artificial (virtual) or contrived change for the sake of change. It cannot be bought over the counter nor in a psychotherapy office, although it may include these. In the biblical sense wholeness includes possibilities for deep and comprehensive conversion from one state into a superior one that is more oriented toward God's purposes. Healing is a dynamic of this transforming wholeness. Healing, in the wholeness sense, is more than one person getting well or a single organ transplant. It is all of us getting well in some way together. When we participate in wholeness we can discern what is needed in transformation, and when it is occurring. Spiritual leaders can even function as agents of wholeness and transformation. This is one of the joys of pastoring (Rom. 12:1-2).

How do sexuality and sex fit into wholeness? Sexuality fits well, for it is already a part of wholeness. Sex fits, if those acting out their sexuality are healthy in body-mind-spirit.

Our working definition of sexuality is that it is a gift of God: it is a function of spirituality, it includes a gender polarity, it is generative, and it is relational. Sexuality then, by definition, is a part of healthiness. It fits God's purposes. And sexuality is transformative that is, it has the power not only to generate new life but also the power to change life moderately or dramatically. Like God's other gifts, sexuality can be used for good or ill, for pleasure or wantonness, to enhance or abuse, to create or destroy. One must wonder again at the purposes of the Creator in giving humankind such a potent gift with so little built-in wisdom for handling it. There is reassurance, however, in noting that the vast majority of the geofamily manage their sexuality reasonably well.

For the sincere religious believer the starting place is the sacredness of sexuality, for it is a gift of God. Further, there is the stewardship factor. It is a gift rather than a possession. We are accountable to God and all of creation for how we manage this gift. Yet again because it is a gift of God, it is a positive gift, capable of creating and providing deep enjoyment. And because sexuality is a function of spirituality, it is relational. For all of creation is spiritual. Humankind does best when it expresses sexuality in terms of caring relationships.

The interrelationship of sexuality and spirituality can be stated in another way, as Joan Timmerman does with the premise of her book, *The Mardi Gras Syndrome* (1984): "human sexuality can function in human lives as a sacramental reality, the spiritual significance of our sexual lives and the sexual significance of our spiritual lives need not remain a 'forgotten' theological truth" (quoted in Timmerman 1992, 1).

In organized religion we cannot ignore or escape the massive load of traditions and rules meant to control human sexuality. With both sincere devotion, and malice aforethought, our forebears sought to guard us all—and apparently God—from the dark side of human free will. The effect has been to stifle much of the creativity and pleasure that God intended. This leaves "sinners having all the fun," while believers must be satisfied with the missionary position or be sneaky or abusive in search of what should be healthy creativity and pleasure. In this day of social "liberations," more and more people are making their own rules, and learning by consequences. A recent survey of Catholic parishioners indicated that 64 percent didn't know—or ignored—sexual restrictions regarding contraception and abortion when it suited their purposes. We already know that the age for a first sexual experience among youth gets lower, and that many couples coming to religious leaders for weddings have had prior sexual experience. Does organized religion have a responsibility to keep making doctrines that the majority ignore, in hopes of controlling a few? Or should it reformulate teachings so they conform to consensus? It seems likely that we will change by accretion and fear, still trying to dam the deep river of testosterone and estrogen. Perhaps God will give us a transforming opportunity, such as occurred at the Jerusalem Council in Acts 15. Maybe that time is here.

Our working definition of sex is that it is our individual and relational acting out of our gift of sexuality. Sex is literally an abbreviation for sexuality. This means that sex is sexuality writ small. A great and potent gift is put in the hands of mortals with limited insight and powerful passions. Now that sex is so public, we are seeing its dark side in frightening, depressing detail. Organized religion is struggling so hard to control its resident offenders, and pay for their damage, that it has little energy left over to be creative. Further, sex is now politicized, making consensus unlikely. It is clear that codes of conduct and carefully crafted statements concerning the nobility of love and sexuality are only a beginning of what is needed. Perhaps it is up to the mass of sincere believers to take more responsibility for shaping definitions and policies regarding sexuality and sex. This seems to be occurring.

It is dawning on many of us that spirituality, sexuality, and health are much bigger than we think, compared to our normal condition. We will have to think bigger thoughts and open ourselves to greater realities if we expect to participate in the awesomeness of God's generative Spirit in the new age. And yet each day, each person, and each experience is simply another opportunity to enjoy God's generative creation. For we do not have to be God, we have only to be faithful in stewardship. And faithfulness is essentially a simple, reverent, loving acceptance of our Creator's purposes for us.

What Are Health and Fitness?

Health is a well-known word that isn't known. As mentioned earlier, health has become another word for normal. So health for many means living and acting as one usually does. The presicknesses of our normal lifestyles are becoming clearer, and the enormous costs are a wake-up call. A growing number of people are aware now that how we eat, exercise, drink, think, pray—and do sex—has a major impact on our lives. A segment of our population helping to lead the national crusade for health is the "gym rats," who exercise regularly—and sometimes obsessively. This crusade needs all the leaders it can get. We know from experience that when a critical mass is reached in a large group, the balance of behavior tips in a new direction. How appropriate for organized religion to add its numbers, and its spiritual insights to the national crusade for health and fitness. Those already participating know the wonderful benefits of physical-mental-spiritual fitness. When fit, we feel better, we look better, we work better, we play better, we relate better, and fitness costs less than sickness. We can even note the ripple effect of fitness in a group. Health and fitness are as contagious as sickness.

I am now shifting the key word for this discussion from health to fitness. Health is a fine, inclusive word. But it is too loaded with our subconscious ideas of what is normal to serve us as we recognize our need to break out of our normal thinking and lifestyles in order to be truly healthy. Other terms, such as well being, and wholeness, were noted earlier. These are helpful also. Yet the term that comes closest to a new vision of our bodies, minds, and spirits is fitness.

Fitness, too, has ideational baggage. For to some it means big muscles, running marathons, or physical beauty. The best meaning of fitness is a body-mind-spirit functioning as God intended— "being the best that we can be." No, this is not a call for supererogation, or more mega-pastors. Fitness is simply an open invitation for us to "lay aside every weight and the sin that clings so closely, and let us run with perseverance the race that is set before us" (Heb. 12:1). Not only is fitness an invitation to lay down unhealthy habits and expectations, it is also an invitation to learn "the abundant life" Jesus promised (John 10:10). Even though many of us get caught up in the American illusion that bigger, newer, and faster is better, we know in our heart of hearts that God calls us to a life of fitness for ministry. And the life of fitness is joyful, not burdensome.

Fitness is a way of life, a satisfying way of life. For more information consult my book *Fit to Be a Pastor: A Call to Physical, Mental, and Spiritual Fitness* (2000). Since this word may need some new thinking for those want to develop a "fitness quest," the ABCs method of investigating a subject may be useful. This is my favorite investigation formula.

The ABCs for Exploring Fitness

A = Awareness. What do I know, and need to know, about fitness?
- Why do I need to know this (my "vision," "quest")?
- Where can I find what I need to know?

B = Basics. What are the basic (necessary) experiences and resources needed for this project?
- Clear away misinformation, distractions, and counter-productive habits.
- Develop a plan of action, including goals.
- Gather necessary resources.
- Make necessary decisions.
- Begin. . . .

C = Connections. What are the necessary connections and relationships necessary for this project and for well being?
- Connect necessary lines of communication and information.
- Relate this project to God's call (mission) and stewardship.
- Activate or build an appropriate support system.
- Share failures and successes with appropriate persons.

Getting fit and developing a healthy/fit lifestyle is well worth considerable effort. To break the inertia (habitual thought patterns, resistance, misinformation) that reinforces our unhealthiness, we need a convincing reason for these changes (I have tried to provide some), the courage to follow God's Holy Spirit into "transformation" (Rom. 12:1, 2) and a mature discipline of body-mind-spirit.

Discipline: Cornerstone of Fitness

"Discipline" is not a four-letter word. And it is not a boring pain. That illusion is part of the inertia that makes change difficult for some. We have a natural and strong desire to be comfortable (no pain) and secure (no changes). The good news is that when we become fit we will be comfortable—in fact very pleased with ourselves and secure, for we will handle changes more confidently.

A working definition of discipline, as used here, is "positive self-management." Negative self-management occurs when we do not guide our lives by reliable reference points. It also means guiding our lives by habits that do not lead to positive results. Self-management is what we do with our lives all the time, whether we realize this or not. So this simple definition of discipline suggests that we become more conscious of where our habits are leading us. And it suggests that we keep managing ourselves as we were doing anyway, except that we change what is not leading to fitness. That's not drudgery, it's just good common sense.

I value Peter M. Senge's simple yet profound definition of discipline in his book, *The Fifth Discipline* (1990): "A discipline is a developmental path for acquiring certian skills or competencies" (10). He goes on throughout this book to demonstrate the value of pursuing such a path.

Another term for discipline is habits. Much of our life is run by our habits—when we get up in the morning, how we eat, what we do for recreation, how we pray, and such. Habits are valuable when they are positive. For we save energy and time when we do not have to figure out what we will do next, or how we will do it.

Yet another term for discipline is attitude. This is our mental-spiritual ability to shape our thinking and behavior with a single definitive thought. Viktor Frankl, the Austrian psychiatrist, turned psychoanalytic theory upside down after World War II, when he shared what he had discovered in the Nazi death camps. He told how he watched so many die in anguish, while a few survived. Many of those who survived, including himself, did so primarily through their attitudes. The attitude was a conscious drive toward positive meaning in their lives. No matter what is happening, such persons put negative (meaningless) thoughts out of their minds and focus instead on making their lives have positive meaning—by their thinking, by their habits, and by their service to others.

The disciplines that make such a life possible begin with a simple declaration of what meaning a person wants their life to have, then living it. Such disciplines are easier than rules, for they contain good enough reasons to continue. Frankl (1963) called this kind of thinking "logotherapy." It predates many of the contemporary positive thinking movements.

Finally, another term for discipline is stewardship. Disciplined fitness is not just about an individual, it is about all of us. When body-mind-spirit fitness orders our lives, stewardship is not just an add-on or another guilt-trip. Stewardship becomes our sacred trust. We can see, feel, and enjoy it in our bodies, our minds, our spirits. James B. Nelson (1978) calls this "embodiment" (incarnation)—a most appropriate designation. For additional development of the spiritual aspect of disciplines, see Richard J. Foster (1978) and Dallas Willard (1988).

For pastors who want their lives to be dedicated to the meaning of pastoral ministry, the disciplines of fitness will be developed and sustained by this very positive attitude. The habits by which such a pastor lives are habits that keep her or him living in a fitness that produces ministry for others and the deep joys of ministry for the pastor. Fitness is also an "adventure" (remember that word?). It is a spiritual adventure of body-mind-spirit in which a person explores, through positive habits, how good a person and pastor she can become.

The Positive Regimen for Body-Mind-Spirit Fitness

As with so many good undertakings, the fitness adventure as a great idea is simple. It's the *doing* of it that may become complicated, unless we keep it simple. Five dynamic guidelines can make fitness a reality:

- eat smart
- exercise more
- drink water
- think free
- pray high

Eat smart means taking time to think about eating habits. Thinking we don't have time to think about eating is an excuse. We think about it a lot, whether we are conscious of this or not. Make a point of thinking consciously of each meal of the day, as well as healthier ways to plan and prepare them. This works best when partners or a family learn to do this together. Learn to listen to your body, for it has ways of telling you what it needs, and how much. A clear rule/habit for this is to eat one half as much as you usually do. For according to former U.S. Surgeon General Everett Koop, Americans eat far more than they need for health. When beginning a fitness quest, you may need to eat more often, but always eat less than you want, for it is the need not the want that matters. And yes, you can still eat chocolate—just half as much. This is "the rule of half."

Exercise more means be active—physically, mentally, and spiritually. Our bodies, minds, and spirits are built for action. Sedentariness slows everything down until we can't function healthily. The minimal guideline from experts is to do vigorous activity for half an hour five days per week. This is "the rule of movement."

Drink water means drink more fluid than is typical. Americans drink too little fluid to keep their immune system, mucous membranes, digestive system, brain, and skin healthy. Soda, processed fruit drinks, even milk, are not as useful or inexpensive as water. We need eight glasses of water per day. This is "the rule of eight."

Think free means to turn our minds loose from old habits of thinking that keep us going in circles instead of on an adventure. We were born with curiosity ("I wonder what would happen if I . . ."). Our minds were made to be creative ("I can do this better"), even if we must do it in our imagination. Natural curiosity and creativity can become buried under boring and counterproductive habits. Remember attitude? An attitude of openness to positive possibilities, to ways I can grow, to ways of fulfilling God's purposes better, points us toward fitness. This is "the rule of openness."

Pray high means to pray toward God's higher purposes, instead of for what I think God should do (Isa. 55:9). At spiritual retreats I like to have every one do an analysis of their typical prayers. Typically, we find that most of the prayers are "co-dependent" prayers. That is, we tend to pray for things we must do for ourselves, as if God would miraculously keep us healthy when we continually abuse our bodies, or save us from sexual addictions when we must learn this for ourselves. We can pray for healing, or guidance, or for victims of HIV/AIDS, but we must then be open to God's ways of healing, granting us discernment, or supporting us with grace for ministry to those suffering from AIDS. This makes prayer an active adventure, a partnership with an active, loving God. This is "the rule of amplitude."

How are body-mind-spirit health and fitness connected to sexuality and sex? I pray more and more of us will make this connection. For it is clear that we get sick when we forget how to be well. The prescription is to understand our sicknesses and concentrate on being fit as persons and as spiritual leaders. This kind of health and fitness is one of the best resources for witness and evangelism that I know. For health is as contagious as sickness.

Summary

This chapter begins with an invitation to think of the "light side" of organized religion, after spending much time analyzing and struggling to control its "dark side." The story of the Reverend

Cal Hopkins is presented as a reminder of how important it is to catch ourselves before we cross the shadowy boundaries of sexual misconduct.

Then the light side is explored in a review of God's purposes in the "wholeness" of the geofamily and all of creation. Five principles are then applied to our sexuality and our sexual behavior.

Finally, the contemporary insights and regimens of health and fitness of body-mind-spirit are reviewed, and then summarized in five dynamic guidelines for fitness of person and ministry. Throughout this chapter there is an implied and specific call for organized religion to share in leadership of the emerging national crusade for health and fitness in America.

Appendix

Inventory of Spirituality
and Sexuality

It is not customary to think of sexuality and spirituality together, much less as part of the energy system that drives our lives. It can be useful, therefore, to take some time to identify each of these two dynamics and how they blend.

This inventory of spirituality is not a clinical test. Yet it offers opportunities to think of significant individuals and experiences and to understand how these have blended into a pattern for your life. As you think of these persons and experiences, let your memory connect others with the ones you remember easily. For the pattern is deep and interwoven. It will include items that may have seemed insignificant earlier, yet now can be seen more clearly in hindsight. When this inventory exercise is done in relaxed meditation, it is likely that God's Holy Spirit will offer discernment for the meanings in your pattern. And if you see factors that need further meditation, set a time to do so. If you sense factors that indicate serious complications, you will find it valuable to examine them in prayer, and with a pastoral counselor, spiritual director, or competent mentor.

The terms "spiritual" and "sexual" have some common meanings and some personal meanings for you. The responses to the inventory items will be most meaningful for you if you respond to the items from your personal meanings.

This inventory includes an essay section and a set of statements designed for use in brief research settings, with a counselor, a study group, or a research project. You will need additional writing paper or a journal for your responses to the essay questions and your reactions to the research questions.

A note of caution: Participation in the use of this inventory is completely voluntary. It contains probing questions and ideas that are not intended to induce embarrassment, pain, or anger. Their value lies in aiding an understanding of deep-seated memories and patterns of experience. If you feel upset as you respond to the inventory issues, stop your work with the inventory and consider whether or not you wish to proceed later, or not at all. If you feel deeply disturbed responding to any of these inventory issues or memories associated with them, end your responses immediately and find competent professional assistance in dealing with your reactions.

Items marked with an asterisk (*) indicate possible need for professional counsel.

Regarding confidentiality: Persons writing responses to any items in this inventory are urged to write them on paper that can be kept confidential, under your control, and shared with others only if you choose to do so.

Essay Issues

1. Please write your definition of spirituality.

*2. List some of your earliest memories of spiritual experiences and how they affected you.

3. List persons most influential in your spiritual development, and how each one affected you.

*4. Please indicate whether or not you have ever heard God speaking to you in actual words.

5. List major experiences in your life, and how these affected you spiritually.

6. List the persons, experiences, and feelings you are most afraid of spiritually.

7. Describe the importance of attending church in your spiritual experience.

8. Compare the value for you of having spiritual experiences alone or in groups.

9. If you have a spiritual director, please explain why this is important to you.

10. List and compare religious symbols (cross, candle, etc.) and experiences (prayer, grief, etc.) of spirituality importance to you, and why you value them.

11. List ways you relate to the persons of the Christian Trinity—God, Creator, Jesus Christ, Savior, Holy Spirit, Sustainer.

*12. Describe your beliefs about sin, evil, and death, and how they affect you.

13. Describe your beliefs about and experiences of spiritual healing.

14. Describe your "sacred spaces" for meditation, and how you use them.

15. Describe how you feel spiritually related to this planet.

16. List ways your spirituality has changed over the years.

17. Describe how you express your spirituality in your daily lifestyle.

*18. Describe how your spirituality affects your close relationships.

*19. Write what changes you would like to have in your spirituality.

20. Describe how you expect those changes to happen.

21. Discuss the patterns of spirituality you see now in your life.

22. What are your definitions of "sexuality" and "sex"?

*23. Describe your experiences with pornography.

24. Describe how your happiest experiences of sexuality and spirituality relate to each other.

25. How would you like to change the relationship between your spirituality and your sexuality?

Research Issues

Circle one response for each item.

1. Definition: Spirituality is God's dynamic love in action.

| Strongly Agree | Agree | Uncertain | Disagree | Strong Disagree |

2. My earliest memories of spiritual experiences are pleasant.

| Strongly Agree | Agree | Uncertain | Disagree | Strong Disagree |

*3. I was taught to be afraid of God and Satan when I was a child.

| Strongly Agree | Agree | Uncertain | Disagree | Strong Disagree |

4. I have loved going to church and religious events since childhood.

| Strongly Agree | Agree | Uncertain | Disagree | Strong Disagree |

5. No one taught me about spiritual issues in my childhood or youth.

| Strongly Agree | Agree | Uncertain | Disagree | Strong Disagree |

*6. I feel guilty that I don't do more for God and the church.

| Strongly Agree | Agree | Uncertain | Disagree | Strong Disagree |

7. I had a conversion experience in adulthood that changed my life.

| Strongly Agree | Agree | Uncertain | Disagree | Strong Disagree |

*8. I had a pastor who engaged in sexual misconduct with someone and was deposed.

| Strongly Agree | Agree | Uncertain | Disagree | Strong Disagree |

9. I believe sex and spirituality are private matters.

Strongly   Agree   Uncertain   Disagree   Strong
Agree   Disagree

10. I believe appropriate intimate relationships include an empha-
    sis on healthy spirituality and healthy sexuality.

Strongly   Agree   Uncertain   Disagree   Strong
Agree   Disagree

   The value of this inventory will be most apparent if you take
time to think about your responses. Look for patterns of thought
and behavior that show an influence on present thinking and emotions. Look for issues that are exceptionally uncomfortable and
seek professional assistance in examining them. And consider
what your responses suggest for your healthy future.

WORKS CITED

Berridge, Kent C. "Pleasures of the Brain." 2003. *Brain & Cognition* 52 (10): 106–28.

Bonhoeffer, Dietrich. 1959. *The Cost of Discipleship*. New York: Macmillan.

Boswell, John. 1980. *Christianity, Social Tolerance, and Homosexuality: Gay People in Western Europe from the Beginning of the Christian Era to the Fourteenth Century*. Chicago: University of Chicago Press.

Carnes, Patrick. 1994. *Out of the Shadows: Understanding Sexual Addiction*. Center City, Minn.: Hazelden.

Carroll, Jackson W., Barbara Hargrove, and Adair T. Lummis 1983. *Women of the Cloth: A New Opportunity for the Churches*. San Francisco: Harper and Row.

Carroll, Matt, Kevin Cullen, Thomas Farragher, Stephen Kurkjian, Michael Paulson, Sacha Pfeiffer, Michael Rezendes, and Walter V. Robinson (investigative staff of the *Boston Globe*). 2002. *Betrayal: The Crisis in the Catholic Church*. Boston: Little, Brown.

Christian Ministry Resources. Church Law and Tax Report. www.churchlawtoday.com.

Clinebell, Howard. 1992. *Well Being: A Personal Plan for Exploring and Enriching the Seven Dimensions of Life*. San Francisco: Harper San Francisco.

———. 1996. *Ecotherapy: Healing Ourselves, Healing the Earth*. Minneapolis: Fortress Press.

Cooper-White, Pamela. 1995. *The Cry of Tamar: Violence against Women and the Church's Response*. Minneapolis: Fortress Press.

D'Antonio, William V. 2002. Cited in "Rebels in the Pews" by David Van Biema, *Time* (June 17).

Department of Justice. 1998. "National Violence against Women Survey."

Dodson, Betty. 1996. *Sex for One: The Joy of Self-Loving.* New York: Three Rivers Press.

Evans, Abigail Rian. 1999. *The Healing Church: Practical Programs for Health Ministries.* Cleveland: United Church Press.

Fortune, Marie. *Clergy Sexual Misconduct: Sexual Abuse in the Ministerial Relationship.* 1997. Workshop manual. Seattle: Center for the Prevention of Sexual and Domestic Violence.

————. 1999. *Is Nothing Sacred? The Story of a Pastor, the Women He Sexually Abused, and the Congregation He Nearly Destroyed.* Cleveland: United Church Press.

Foster, Richard J. 1978. *Celebration of Discipline: The Path to Spiritual Growth.* New York: Harper and Row.

Fox, Matthew. 1983. *Original Blessing.* Santa Fe: Bear & Co.

————. 1999. *Sins of the Spirit, Blessings of the Flesh.* New York: Three Rivers Press.

Frankl, Viktor E. 1963. *Man's Search for Meaning: An Introduction to Logotherapy.* Translated by Ilse Lasch. New York: Washington Square Press, 1963.

Friberg, Nils, and Mark Laaser. 1998. *Before the Fall: Preventing Pastoral Sexual Abuse.* Collegeville, Minn.: Order of St. Benedict.

Gilson, Anne Bathurst. 1995. *Eros Breaking Free: Interpreting Sexual Theo-Ethics.* Cleveland: Pilgrim.

Goleman, Daniel. 1995. *Emotional Intelligence.* New York: Bantam.

Greeley, Andrew. 1979. *Crisis in the Church: A Study of Religion in America.* Chicago: Thomas More.

Gustafson, James M. 1984. *Ethics from a Theocentric Perspective,* vol. 2. Chicago: University of Chicago Press.

Heyward, Carter. 1995. *Staying Power: Reflections on Gender, Justice, and Compassion.* Cleveland: Pilgrim Press.

214 Works Cited

Howard, Pierce J. 2000. *The Owner's Manual for the Brain: Everyday Applications from Mind-Brain Research*. Austin: Bard.

Hunter, Rodney J., gen. ed. 1990. *Dictionary of Pastoral Care and Counseling*. Nashville: Abingdon.

Johnson, Brad, and William Johnson. 2000. *The Pastor's Guide to Psychological Disorders and Treatments*. New York: Haworth.

Jung, Carl G. *Man and His Symbols*. 1964. Garden City, N.Y.: Doubleday.

Knauer, Sandra. 2002. *Recovering from Sexual Abuse, Addictions, and Compulsive Behaviors*. New York: Haworth.

Lindner, Eileen W., ed. 2002. *Yearbook of American and Canadian Churches 2000*. Nashville: Abingdon.

Livingston, David J. 2002. *Healing Violent Men: A Model for Christian Communities*. Minneapolis: Fortress Press.

MacLean, Paul. 1984. Cited in *Whole-Brain Thinking: Working from Both Sides of the Brain to Achieve Peak Job Performance* by Jacquelyn Wonder and Pricilla Donovan. New York: Ballantine.

McClintock, Karen A. 2001. *Sexual Shame: An Urgent Call to Healing*. Minneapolis: Fortress Press.

Moir, Anne, and David Jessel. 1991. *Brain Sex: The Real Difference between Men and Women*. New York: Carol.

Money, John. 1981. *Love and Love Sickness: The Science of Sex, Gender Difference, and Pair-Bonding*. Baltimore: Johns Hopkins University Press.

———. 1999. *The Lovemap Guidebook: A Definitive Statement*. New York: Continuum.

Moore, G. E. 1903. *Principia Ethica*. Cambridge: Cambridge University Press.

Morris, Debbie, with Gregg Lewis. 1998. *Forgiving the Dead Man Walking*. Grand Rapids, Mich.: Zondervan.

Morrison, James R. 2001. *DSM-IV Made Easy: The Clinician's Guide to Diagnosis*. New York: Guilford.

Muller, James. 2002. Cited in "Rebels in the Pews" by David Van Biema. *Time* (June 17).

Nelson, James B. 1978. *Embodiment: An Approach to Sexuality and Christian Theology.* Minneapolis: Augsburg.

————. 1986. *Between Two Gardens: Reflections on Sexuality and Religious Experience.* Westminster John Knox.

————. 1992. *Body Theology.* Louisville: Westminster John Knox.

Neuger, Christie Cozad. 2001. *Counseling Women: A Narrative, Pastoral Approach.* Minneapolis: Fortress Press.

Niebuhr, H. Richard. 1951. *Christ and Culture.* New York, Harper.

Ó Murchú, Diarmuid. 1997. *Quantum Theology.* New York: Crossroad.

Paulson, Michael. 2002. "Vatican Stance on Gay Clergy Criticized" (March 4). Cited by Mary Ann Tolbert in a special report from the Center for Lesbian and Gay Studies, Pacific School of Religion, Berkeley.

Polkinghorne, John. 1996. *Quarks, Chaos and Christianity: Questions to Science and Religion.* New York: Crossroad.

Ratey, John J. 2001. *A User's Guide to the Brain: Perception, Attention, and the Four Theaters of the Brain.* New York: Pantheon.

Ratey, John J., and Catherine Johnson. 1997. *Shadow Syndromes.* New York: Bantam.

Rediger, G. Lloyd. 1982. *Coping with Clergy Burnout.* Valley Forge, Penn.: Judson Press.

————. 1990. *Ministry and Sexuality: Cases, Counseling, and Care.* Minneapolis: Fortress Press.

————. 2000. *Fit to Be a Pastor: A Call to Physical, Mental, and Spiritual Fitness.* Louisville: Westminster John Knox.

Ridley, Matt. 1993. *The Red Queen: Sex and the Evolution of Human Nature.* New York: Penguin.

Rogers, Carl R. 1961. *On Becoming a Person.* Boston: Houghton Mifflin.

Rosetti, Stephen J. 1996. *A Tragic Grace: The Catholic Church and Child Sexual Abuse.* Collegeville, Minn.: Liturgical Press.

Russell, Letty M., and Shannon Clarkson, eds. 1996. *Dictionary of Feminist Theologies.* Louisville: Westminster John Knox.

Schneider, Jennifer, and Robert Weiss. 2001. *Cybersex Exposed: Simple Fantasy or Obsession?* Center City, Minn.: Hazelden.

Schwab, Charlotte Rolnick. 2002. *Sex, Lies, and Rabbis: Breaking a Sacred Trust.* Bloomington, Ind.: 1st Books.

Segal, Erich. 1970. *Love Story.* New York: HarperCollins.

Senge, Peter M. 1990. *The Fifth Discipline: The Art and Practice of Learning Organization.* New York: Doubleday.

Sipe, Richard A. W. 2002. Quoted in the *Boston Globe,* "Vatican Stance on Gay Clergy Criticized" (March 4) by Michael Paulson, cited by Mary Ann Tolbert in a special report from the Center for Lesbian and Gay Studies, Pacific School of Religion, Berkeley.

Sweet, Leonard I. 1999. *Aqua Church.* Loveland, Colo.: Group.

Timmerman, Joan. 1984. *The Mardi Gras Syndrome: Rethinking Christian Sexuality.* New York: Crossroad.

———. 1992. *Sexuality and Spiritual Growth.* New York: Crossroad.

Trull, Joe E. and James E. Carter. 1993. *Ministerial Ethics: Being a Good Minister in a Not-So-Good World.* Nashville: Broadman and Holman.

Van Biema, David. "Rebels in the Pews." 2002. *Time* (June 17).

Van Dam, Carla. 2001. *Identifying Child Molesters: Preventing Child Sexual Abuse.* New York: Haworth.

Weldon, T. D. 1945. *Introduction to Kant's* Critique of Practical Reason. Oxford: Oxford University Press.

Wilbur, Ken. 2000. *Sex, Ecology, Spirituality: The Spirit of Evolution.* Boston: Shambhala.

Willard, Dallas. 1988. *The Spirit of the Disciplines: Understanding How God Changes Lives.* San Francisco: Harper.

Internet resources

www.aasect.org (American Association of Sex Educators, Counselors, and Therapists)
www.advocateweb.org
www.barna.org
www.churchlawtoday.com
www.survivorsfirst.org

ACKNOWLEDGMENTS

With thankfulness I acknowledge many who have shared their stories, insights, critiques, and encouragement in the development of this book. Though my long experience in dealing with clergy sexual misconduct is the basis of this writing, its authenticity, sensitivity, and scholarly perceptions are influenced by gracious and knowledgeable professionals and advocates.

I am indebted to Fortress Press for permission to use material from my earlier book for them, entitled *Ministry and Sexuality: Cases, Counseling and Care* (1990), and especially to Michael West and Marshall Johnson for wise editorial guidance, and to Zan Ceeley, my production editor at Fortress.

Generous financial support from the Louisville Institute made the multiple interviews for this book possible.

The Reverend James B. Nelson, Ph.D., Professor Emeritus of Christian Ethics, United Theological Seminary–Twin Cities, New Brighton, Minnesota, has been a career-long mentor and friend to me. His prophetic insights and teachings regarding the celebration of sexuality, a contemporary perspective on sexual ethics, and the relationship between sexuality and spirituality have been an ongoing source of guidance for my thoughts and writings on this subject.

Gary Schoener, Ph.D., Director of the Walk-In Counseling Center, Minneapolis, is a premier researcher and historian of sexual misconduct by mental health professionals and clergy. Besides being a pioneering counselor for victim-survivors, he is generous in sharing his experience and data with advocates, trainers, and other researchers.

I am deeply grateful for personal interviews in which Gary brought me back up to speed on the sexual misconduct patterns and data, after I had been pursuing other issues for several years.

Marie Fortune, a pioneer in addressing sexual abuse and domestic violence, was also generous with her time and insights. Her courageous and prophetic leadership continues to be a benchmark in calling the church to justice and integrity. Through her Center for Prevention of Sexual and Domestic Violence in Seattle, she now produces award-winning training films and organizes training conferences designed to prevent the abuses she has probed for so many years. She has an able associate in Rabbi Cindy Enger.

The Reverend Homer U. Ashby Jr., Ph.D., Professor of Pastoral Care at McCormick Theological Seminary, gave me the generous gift of an introduction into the African-American community of Chicago. In addition to offering his scholarly insights into the African-American clergy scene, he also introduced me to the Reverend Calvin Morris, Ph.D., Executive Director of the Community Renewal Society, Chicago's pioneering community service organization, and to the Reverend Sharon Ellis, D.Min., a dynamic advocate, counselor, and trainer for women abused by black pastors. Interviews with these three church and community leaders provided valuable insights for this book.

Archbishop Michael Sheehan of the Archdioceses of Santa Fe, New Mexico, granted me one of the first interviews for this book. The archbishop has been a notable leader in dealing with priestly sexual misconduct and in developing the zero-tolerance policy for malfeasant Catholic clergy. His insights regarding the reason priests fall into moral misconduct have helped shape my perspective.

Louis McBurney, M.D., and Melissa McBurney gave me an extended interview in the picturesque retreat center in the mountains above Marble, Colorado, a place where many troubled pastors and spouses have found healing and guidance from these extraordinary counselors and trainers of trainers. The McBurneys have set a standard for being God's agents in transforming and supporting evangelical clergy. Even those of us with long experience continue to learn from their model.

Rabbi Arthur Gross-Schaefer, J.D., Professor in the Business College, Loyola Marymount University, Los Angeles, has been generous in discussing the rabbinical scene in Judaism. His writings on ethics and his training in scandal management have provided valuable insights.

The Reverend Christie Cozad Neuger, Ph.D., Professor of Pastoral Care and Theology at United Theological Seminary–Twin Cities, New Brighton, Minnesota, provided a stimulating interview highlighting the abuse and recovery of women in organized religion. Her book on this theme offers thought-provoking and useful insights on the causes, remedies, and the healthy roles of women.

Joan H. Timmerman, Ph.D., Professor Emerita, College of St. Catherine, St. Paul, Minnesota, has written breakthrough books on the relationship of sexuality and spirituality. E-mail conversations with her have helped inform my theology of sexual spirituality.

The Reverend Nils Friberg, Ph.D., Professor of Pastoral Theology, Bethel College and Seminary (ret.), St. Paul, Minnesota, has been a friend and colleague for some years. Our frank exchanges and insights have been especially useful in the writing of this book, for clergy sexual morality is a major theme of his teaching and writing.

The Reverend Bruce M. Hartung, Ph.D., Director of Clergy Support Ministries, Lutheran Church Missouri Synod, is a wise and innovative pioneer in realistic and genuinely caring support and training programs for clergy. Our conversations and shared leadership events continue to stimulate valuable insights for clergy support programs.

The Reverend David C. Parachini, Nathan Network Convener, Grace Episcopal Church, Windsor, Connecticut, shared phone and e-mail time with me regarding the Nathan Network and the Safe Church Training programs. Our conversations took place too late to be included in this book, but his insights, and the programs he convenes are extraordinary resources for managing and preventing clergy sexual misconduct.

The Reverend Stephen Rosetti, Director of St. Luke Institute, a treatment center specializing in therapy for priests, in Silver Spring, Maryland, gave generous assistance, not only with suggestions regarding clergy therapy but also in sharing two professional papers delivered to the Association for the Treatment of Sexual Abusers conference in October 2001.

Presbyterian Chaplain James S. Evinger offered helpful suggestions for the preparation of this book. He makes a valuable contribution to the literature on clergy sexual misconduct through a newsletter and the maintenance of an exhaustive bibliography at website: www.advocateweb.org/hope/bibliographyje/default.asp.

The Reverend Barbara Dua, D. Min., Executive Director of the New Mexico Conference of Churches, and formerly Director of Women's Ministries, Presbyterian Church (U.S.A.), brings extraordinary leadership skills and insights to her prominent roles in organized religion. She is always generous in sharing these gifts in our relationship.

The Reverend James E. Large, of the New Mexico Conference, United Methodist Church, provided valuable explanations and perspectives on clergy sexual misconduct, as treated in the UMC document, *Living the Sacred Trust: Clergy Sexual Ethics* and as a supplant to the UMC's *The Book of Discipline*.

The Reverend Kay B. Huggins, D. Min., pastor, teacher, trainer, has provided numerous opportunities for sincere and spiritually challenging conversations regarding the role of women in organized religion and the changing roles of clergy in society. Her insights and teachings are valued wherever she serves.

A supportive host of colleagues and friends have been encouraging and extraordinarily helpful with professional feedback, research, administrative assistance, and deeply appreciated friendship: Howard Clinebell, Ph.D.; James Logan, Ph.D.; the Reverend

James M. Collie; the Reverend David C. Brown; the Reverend Roger Cantril, D. Rel. (deceased); Robbie Buell, a tireless transcriber; Jim Cook, M.B.A., a persistent researcher; Jeanne Maruska, long-time friend and former confidential administrative associate; the Reverend Bill Wineke, religion editor, *Wisconsin State Journal*; and Brian Dunn of Euroclydon Industries, a most competent computer technician, who salvaged my crashed computer.

And then there's my cherished family, with Vera Hansen Rediger, beloved marriage partner and colleague in all things thoughtful and beautiful. No man was ever more blessed with such friends, colleagues, and family.

INDEX

dissonant sexual expressions
(continued)
 cybersex, 92–96
 defining, 91
 paraphilias, 96–101
 sexual dysfunctions, 101–4
 sexual harassment, 104–9
Dodson, Betty, 180
Dossey, Larry, 193
drug therapy, 70, 128, 129
DSM-IV (Diagnostic and Statistical Manual-IV)
 on child sexual abuse, 68, 69,
  79, 98
 on incest, 68, 69, 79
 on paraphilias, 97–98
 sexual dysfunction
  classifications, 102–4
 on sexual predators, 79
Duke Divinity School, 32
dysfunctions. *See* Sexual Dysfunctions
dyspareunia, 103–4

*Ecotherapy: Healing Ourselves,
 Healing the Earth* (Clinebell),
 185
Ellis, Sharon, 82
Embodiment (Nelson), 165
emotions
 clergy misconduct and emotional intimidation, 36–37
 gender differences in, 176
 intimacy and, 183
 of victim-survivors, 122–24
ephebophilia
 defining, 56–57, 63, 98
 determining causes of, 64
 neuropsychological
  impairment and, 61–63, 98
 treatment of, 64, 70

See also child sexual abuse;
 pedophilia
Erikson, Erik, 160
erotica
 biblical, 92
 connecting sexuality and
  spirituality, 92–93
 cybersex and, 92
 and Western cultural anxiety,
  93
ethics
 absolutist, 150, 152–54, 155
 of belief, 15, 30
 codes of, 25, 71–72, 109
 of consequences, 15, 30,
  150–52, 154–58
 human behavior and, 150–59
ethics of consequences, 15, 30,
 150–52, 154–58
Evangelical Lutheran Church in
 America (ELCA), 8
Evans, Abigail Ryan, 193
exercise, 197–98, 202. *See also*
 fitness; healthy lifestyles
exercise therapy, 129
exhibitionism, 97
exorcism, 111–12, 129–30

family therapy, 87, 130
female orgasmic disorder, 103
female sexual arousal disorder,
 102
fetishism, 97, 98–101
The Fifth Discipline (Senge), 200
*Fit to Be a Pastor: A Call to
 Physical, Mental, and Spiritual Fitness* (Rediger), 198–99
fitness, 198–203
 ABCs for exploring, 199
 defining, 198–99
 discipline and, 200–201

exercise and, 197–98, 202
guidelines for, 201–3
organized religion and, 198
See also healthy lifestyles and
fitness
forgiveness and reconciliation,
125–26
Fortune, Marie, 7, 35, 73, 74,
79, 107
Foster, Richard J., 201
Fowler, James W., 160, 193
Fox, Matthew, 165, 193
Frankl, Viktor, 200–201
Freud, Sigmund, 140, 160, 165
Friberg, Nils, 7, 84
frotteurism, 97
Fuller Seminary, 9

gay-lesbian sexuality, 180–82.
See also homosexuality
gender differences
human sexuality and, 175–76
in victimhood experiences,
123
Gilson, Anne Bathurst, 11
Goodman, Ellen, 5
Greeley, Andrew, 4
Gregory, Wilton, 6
Gross-Schaeffer, Arthur, 30
group therapy, 87, 128, 130
guidelines for healing, 121–35
applications of therapeutic
models, 131–35
important definitions, 121–27
therapeutic models, 127–30
See also Interventions and
therapies
Gustafson, James M., 160

"halo effect," 32
Hanson, Mark S., 8

harassment. *See* sexual harassment
healing. *See* guidelines for healing;
interventions and therapies
healthy lifestyles and fitness, 19,
187–203
and clergy boundary
violations, 191–92
discipline and, 200–201
exercise and, 197–98, 202
fitness, 198–203
holistic health, 192–93
normalcy and, 188, 197, 198
organized religion and, 193,
196–97, 198
popular definitions of health,
193
principles of biblical
wholeness and, 194–97
unhealthy clergy lifestyles,
32–34, 188–92
healthy sexuality, 163–86
as adventure, 163–64
the brain and sexual pleasure,
11–12, 176–77
creativity of, 172–73
defining sex, 24, 171, 196–97
defining sexuality, 24, 171,
195
erotica and, 92–93
gay-lesbian sex, 180–82
gender differences and,
175–76
generativity of, 173–74
as gift, 167, 195
healthy lifestyles and fitness,
19, 187–203
HIV/AIDS and, 177–79
hormones and, 11
and important generic
definitions, 169–71

healthy sexuality *(continued)*
  intimacy and, 182–84
  Jesus' model and, 174
  love and, 167, 169–71, 172
  masturbation and self-sex,
    179–80
  organized religion and, 193,
    196–97
  planetary sexuality and,
    185–86
  principles of biblical
    wholeness and, 194–97
  sexuality's constant presence,
    9–10, 11–12, 24
  and significant issues of
    spirituality, 175–82
  societal changes and, 139
  spiritual sexuality and
    theology of, 165–75, 195–97
  theological premises of
    spiritual sexuality, 172–75
  transformation and, 168, 195
Heyward, Carter, 182
HIV/AIDS, 177–79, 188, 203
Hoge, Dean, 5
homosexuality
  Catholic priesthood and, 5
  clergy sex scandals and, 5, 18
  gay-lesbian sexuality, 180–82
  pedophilia and, 5, 18, 64
Hopkins, Cal, 189–92
Hopkins, Nancy, 7
human behavior, psychology of,
  139–62
  anger and, 141, 145, 146, 149
  conscience and, 160–61
  ethics and, 150–59
  extroverts and, 143, 145, 147
  fear and, 141–42, 143, 144,
    149
  identity agenda, 141–42,

    145–46, 149
  intimacy and, 143–44,
    145–46, 148
  introverts and, 143, 145, 147
  joy and, 141, 146–48, 148
  love and, 141, 145, 146, 149
  pleasure seeking and, 141,
    142, 143, 144, 149
  relationship agenda, 141–42,
    146–49
  sadness and, 141, 146–48,
    147–48
  schemas/agendas for human
    motivations, 140–50
  survival agenda, 141–45, 149
  See also emotions
hypoactive sexual desire disorder,
  102
hypoxyphilia, 97

incest, 65–68
  case study, 65–68
  characteristics of offenders,
    68–69
  child sexual abuse and, 58,
    65–68, 70
  defining, 68
  effects on victim-survivors, 69
  intervention and therapy for,
    70
  women abusers, 69
  See also child sexual abuse
insurance policies, 7, 13
Internet database of abusers, 5.
  See also cybersex
intervention plans, 131–35
  assessment and diagnosis, 131
  care of perpetrator, 131
  debriefing the situation, 132
  establishing long-term plans,
    132

About the Author

The Reverend Dr. G. Lloyd Rediger served as pastor to congregations in Illinois, Minnesota, and Wisconsin before completing his doctoral work in pastoral counseling at the Chicago Theological Seminary. He founded the Office of Pastoral Services for Pastors of the Midwest. He has served on the Board of Directors of three state Conferences for Churches and Editorial Boards of two professional journals. Six books and frequent contributions to religious periodicals have generated large audiences for his creative seminars, seminary lectures, and training events. Presently he lives in Albuquerque, New Mexico, and has a son, daughter-in-law, and granddaughter in California. His avocations are the quantum sciences, the arts, sports, and world travel.

Rediger brings a pastor's heart and a disciplined mind to issues of spiritual leadership. After years as a pastor, and as a pastoral counselor to clergy and their families, Rediger offers his insights and research to denominational offices, seminaries, spiritual leaders, and international audiences. He may be contacted at his website www. members.aol.com/glrediger.